I've Come This Far to Say Hello

Poems Selected and New

I've Come This Far to Say Hello
Poems Selected and New

Poems by Kurt Brown

Preface by Stephen Dunn

Tiger Bark Press • Rochester, NY • 2014

Published by Tiger Bark Press,
202 Mildorf Ave., Rochester, NY 14609.

Design by Philip Memmer.

Cover photo by Laure-Anne Bosselaar.

ISBN-13: 978-0-9860445-1-9

CONTENTS

Preface *by Stephen Dunn*   11

The Kiss   17

From *Return of the Prodigals* (1999)

Cartology   21
Bombing the Swarm   23
From the North Sea   24
Alone in a Farmhouse in Iowa   25
The Cynic   27
Hunger   29
Money as Water   30
The Clumsy Contest   31
Film Noir   33
Chanson D'Amour   35
Dace   36
Return of the Prodigals   38

From *More Things in Heaven and Earth* (2002)

Family Gods   43
A Father's Joke   45
Spreading the Word   47
White Middle Class Male   48
Dear Reader, I Mean No Harm   49
Massive   51
Census   52
A New Age   53
Committee to Upgrade Celestial Signs   54
A '49 Merc   56
How It Arrives   57
More Things in Heaven and Earth   58
Fisherman   59
At the Retirement Home for Slang   60
The Good Devil   61

From *Fables from the Ark* (2004)

Gulp! 65

Biography of a Minor Bacteria 66

Captains of Industry 67

Prayer for a Termite 68

Agonistes 69

Distraction 70

En Passant 71

The Priest 72

Prayer 73

From *Future Ship* (2007)

Future Ship 77

Grandma's Rye 79

The Freedom of Escaped Blood 81

The Sitters 83

What Poems Say 85

Town Beach 86

Bluebirds 87

Looney 88

Tattooed Girls 90

The Race 91

I Only Have Eyes for You 93

Road Report 94

Rocket 88 95

Goodnight Texas 96

Serious 99

Diabetes 102

Saved 104

8mm 105

A Hillside in My Youth 106

From *Sincerest Flatteries* (2007)

Of Kim Addonizio 109

Of John Berryman 110

Of Lucie Brock-Broido 111

Of Stephen Dunn 112

Of Carolyn Forché 113

Of Allen Ginsberg 114

Of Ted Kooser 115

Of Thomas Lux 116

Of Sharon Olds 117

Of Charles Simic 118

Of Gerald Stern 119

Of Jean Valentine 120

Of C. K. Williams 121

From *No Other Paradise* (2010)

Mortal Message 125

Knowledge and Ignorance 127

Prime Time 128

Carnal Echo 129

Somebody Else 131

Whatever It Takes 132

Living with the News 133

Snapshot 134

Secrets 136

River 138

Nihilist 140

Address to My Mother 141

This City 142

In Paradise 143

No Other Paradise 144

From *Time-Bound* (2012)

That Street 155

Present Tense 156

About Time 157

Stag Film 158

Friendship 159

Global Warming 160

Forest 162

A Thousand Kim 164

Tomorrow and Tomorrow 169

Love Poem 170

For Miklós Radnóti 171

Melville at the Custom House   172

A Moment   173

Inside Job   174

Some Late Adventures with the Soul   175

From *Corrigan's Compass* (New Poems)

Sleep's Dark and Silent Gate   179

All That Was Meant to Bring Us Together   180

Long Beach Avenue   181

The High Wide Doors of America   182

Another Loony Love Poem   183

Mixed in a Fusion Indistinguishable   184

Road Trip with Stars around My Ankles   186

Retrospective on the Body   187

Is There Anything Else I Can Help You with Today?   188

Great Historical Perspectives   189

Lorca and the Copenhagen School of Physics   190

The Goliath Bird-Eater VS the Human Heart   192

You Have Been Found Wanting   194

Other New Poems

Taking a Stepdaughter to College   197

Karma   199

Where's the Zoo   200

Pan del Muerto   201

Colophon   203

About the Author   207

PREFACE

Kurt Brown was a young 69 when he died on June 16, 2013. It was a shock to all of us who knew him as a friend and envied his trim, vigorous presence and his great generosity. He had called a few weeks before to say he was going in for an operation. I had become used to his calls, and this call seemed not to raise any dire worries. Sometimes his motive was just to just to chat, sometimes to bet on a college football game (no more than $5). The betting was a social act on his part, a way of keeping in touch, because he was a kind of college football innocent, knowing very little about point spreads and Las Vegas odds, which I was acutely aware of. I did not keep this fact from him, but he would choose a team whose name he liked, or had been winning against lesser opponents, and therefore I mostly won our bets. I mention this because in many ways Kurt had an innocence that allowed him to be astounded by the simple things of the world, an innocence that could be useful to a lyric poet. In his early poetry writing life, he didn't know how to turn it into a virtue. But as he grew as a poet, we'd see that innocence become wonderment, which led to greater surprise and discovery. Certainly by his last two or three books he had learned to manage his wonderment.

Our relationship began in 1977 when Kurt invited me to be part of his newly founded Aspen Writer's Conference. As Director of the Conference, he was a pioneer in what has become a commonplace event for American would-be writers: the summer workshop. Perhaps only Bread Loaf and a few others existed at the time. So my first encounter with Kurt was to see him as a poetry enthusiast. And, to be honest, also as a kind of romantic figure. This was, after all, Aspen, Colorado, and Kurt, during the year, tended bar at a famous restaurant where beautiful women were in plentiful supply, which became part of my image of Kurt Brown. It wasn't until many visits later that I realized—and told him so—that such a life could be, and was, a serious distraction to his development as a poet.

Kurt's life changed, profoundly for the better, when Laure-Anne Bosselaar, a beautiful (but this time substantial) woman came to Aspen from Belgium. It would be easy for me to chart her many virtues, but perhaps it's sufficient to say that she enriched his life in ways that both freed and deepened him as a poet. Somehow, however, he remained the Kurt Brown I'd always known and loved. After they married, Kurt was as happy championing her poetry as he was the work of any of his more famous poetry friends. And for good reason: she was very good, writing in English, one of her four languages.

I often felt that Kurt lacked the selfishness of a typical, successful writer. But his love of poetry, in general, became his brand of ambition. He continued to be more interested in others than in himself, as is evident by his editorship of various anthologies. But he and Laure-Anne each had a keen, though different sense of self-protectiveness. Kurt held back the personal in both his daily encounters and in his work, whereas Laure-Anne's apparent outgoingness gave her permission to let us feel intimate with her while she was in the act of telling only what she wanted us to know. When Kurt's poems started to open up, it seemed he had learned from many sources, not just from Laure-Anne's example, ways to risk disclosure without being nakedly confessional. It seemed that his early tendency toward prolixity had been replaced by an ear that knew what and when was enough, and what language—not just information—co-operated with other language. Ultimately, we got necessary details infused with tone. He had discovered his own quiet music; he had learned to accompany himself.

For example, a poem like "Snapshot" from his 2010 book *No Other Paradise,* with its staggered couplets and italicized refrain line that serve to pace and frame the poem's effects, represents a new way of moving in a poem for Brown. Here it is in its entirety:

SNAPSHOT

Ten men on a postcard   clinging to the cables
of Brooklyn Bridge   they look   *one can't help it*

like insects glued to the struts of some unspeakable web

some things will die with us   memories   words
almost everything will die with us unspoken

it's nearly gone   the sound of waves
pummeling the beach   a seagull's sharp demands

a hundred years   if we had them
won't matter   much less the years we've had

those men   suspended in air   dry leaves
caught in a fence before the wind hauls them away

what do *they* say   in their best suits
perched nonchalantly above the flames of the East River
what matters is that we have been here at all

waves heave up and burst in bright concussions of foam
seagulls weave above it   slandering

in the distance   flags of smoke that never touch land

why not speak of what we know
instead of dangling   always   above the ineffable

on the opposite side   no address   no message

what matters is that we have been here at all

so they say   but what does the wind say
after the men are gone   blowing through those empty cables.

A new way of moving, yes, and an eerie kind of prescience as well. It's as if the poet was acutely conscious of his mortality, or he was allowing his normally submerged unconscious to finally do the talking: "*what matters is that we have been here at all.*" The poem is as exquisite as it is economical in its phrasing, and is mysterious in ways that make some earlier Brown poems seem merely denotative. He leaves us with a question that omits its question mark, a suggestion that the wind says nothing—if it says anything at all—that is answerable. But the poem foreshadows his death, a man in his sixties who, of course, would be thinking about such a thing even without immediate cause.

In the same collection, Kurt's poem "Nihilist" playfully flirts with the idea of nothingness. The poem depends on its perfect timing and the ability to sustain a conceit with verve and wit. This is its conclusion:

And he was bound for it, good for it,
nothing's sweet precocious child.
He had never been good at anything,
except nothing. Nothing could take that

away from him. And nothing would.

I would suggest that early on Kurt wasn't capable of pulling off such a poem, even though he had absorbed his Cummings and his Beckett. Maybe the book that preceded *No Other Paradise,* in which he deliberately imitated contemporary writers he admired, prepared him to write "Nihilist." I'm thinking of *Sincerest Flatteries* (2007), which reads as homage more than it does parody, and lives up to its title in every poem. He was practicing the old-fashioned way—the book could be read as a form of apprenticeship.

The editors of this posthumous collection have chosen artfully; if not always in a manner that reflects the body of his work. That is, there are a preponderance of "death" poems chosen from his earlier collections that serve to presage the later poems. "Film Noir" from his first collection *Return of the Prodigals* (1999) seems to prepare us for "Nihilist." The dark "Chanson D'Amour" with its "He doesn't care, / the lover. What's death to one bereft? / Out there nothing but rain; nothing / but mist across the continent." And the even darker title poem from that same collection, would suggest that he was a poet preoccupied by death from the outset. This is how it begins:

> How often have you made love to someone
> because the Angel of Death passed by your door
> throwing an icy shadow over your life—
> just to let you know He's still there
> in case you forgot, in case you thought
> anything had changed in all these decimated centuries.

But I tend not to think of him that singularly. The brilliant title poem from *Future Ship* (2007) is indicative of a mind deeply surveying the vagaries of memory: "The deeper we move into the future, the more we disappear into the past...." And in that same poem his experimentation with form is evident, the longer line facilitating an examination of the claims and statements he makes throughout. Still others assay the natural world and his ambivalent attitudes toward the America he seems to want to love more than he can. As a whole, his work shows us someone dancing on the edges of what to reveal, what to hold back. Kurt was nothing if not a very private man, and his best poems are triumphs over his reticence and the part of him that struggled with boundaries.

Stephen Dunn

THE KISS

That kiss I failed to give you.
How can you forgive me?
The kiss I would have spent on you is still
There, within me. It will probably die there.
But it will be the last of me to die.

For Laure-Anne

FROM *RETURN OF THE PRODIGALS* (1999)

CARTOLOGY

I love those maps, the old ones
bulging with distortion—gigantic rivers,
oceanic lakes, precipitous headlands
that loom out, hundreds of miles
into the sea. I love the way they go blank
and featureless on the far edge
of a page—*Terra Incognita*—the unknown
made palpable but lacking details.
Monsters lurk there, chimeras
wound around themselves,
breathing fire. Always, in a distant
latitude, the furious face of the wind—
lips pursed, cheeks bulging—
spews out its breath in powerful scrolls,
blows a ship onward into
vast grids of Ocean. I love the round maps
that show continents almost touching,
long before they drifted apart.
For me, the maps are real,
actual pictures of the brain, the heart's geography
laid out by living hands—
a river the size of a river in memory
that raged one spring, wrecked boats
and took a week to cross—
a lake the size of boredom that stood
between the wilderness and home.
A range of mountains, walled up
and snarled with clouds, were mountains
of imagination, though men
had seen them, climbed breathlessly
among their peaks and chasms
then returned to Paris, London or Spain
to scrawl their memories

on parchment for a credible king.
The world was measured by experience
and broken bones, and if the trees
stood taller than trees could stand
that was, after all, the forest
they had entered, seen through the eyes
of avarice and fear. I love to run
my fingers over blank provinces,
those white quadrants the mind cannot
enter, waiting for the birth of the first
animal and the new flowers,
shimmering without names.
When they entered them, the men changed
as the world changed, admitting
a new order of things—a bird so blue
it stood out darkly against the sky,
a big-toothed rat that could breathe underwater
and harvest trees. When they entered them
the earth grew vaster
and the future created itself out of the clean
sweep of oblivion. Nothing
has ever been the same again.

BOMBING THE SWARM

This swarm of bees was hanging
from the branch of a tall tree,
a writhing mass that clung together
and swung down like a black bell.

One of the boys, can't remember who,
picked up an apple— it was late August—
51 or 52—and hurled it into the nest:
it came apart in hunks, like a skull exploding,

then recomposed; but we kept hurling apples
and the swarm kept flying apart, flying together,
replay of a bullet entering a man's brain.
Looking back, I realize we couldn't stop,

neither could the bees, we had this frenzy.
That's when I learned how dangerous
I was—so that now when I walk in a field,
my shadow makes crickets hush

and birds fly away in alarm.

FROM THE NORTH SEA

Here is the shell you brought back,
enigmatic and small. I place it
on my desk and stare. Such a bright thing
to come from that dark water, that cold sea.
Colder than the fury of a young prince
in his domain.
                 I look inside:
the marble walls are flushed with violet
from a hidden source of light
beyond the great chamber. The voice
of policy and worship, even the cries
of execution are still. But not the sound
of water building its white dynasties.

The outer shell is dirty, clotted
with mud from the ocean.
Everywhere the peasant's thin ridges
and furrows, ripples of smoke
from old wars. The landscape is terraced,
rows that follow the pitch of hills
like contour lines on a map.

But where is the tender inhabitant
brought naked and shivering to the gallows?
Hold it up to your ear and listen:

Can you hear the tumult? The crying?
the constant murmur of lost prayers?

for Laure-Anne

ALONE IN A FARMHOUSE IN IOWA

The furnace in the basement groans
like a sick god.
I draw curtains on a night
blackbirds brought,
straw by straw, and stuffed
into walls. Now
crickets rattle in the yard—
and stop—
and rattle—and cars go by
sighing.

The great spaces of America
full of loneliness and raccoons!
Beyond Chicago
the land opens like a prayer.
I have come here
on steps no heavier than dew
to lay my body in a farmhouse in a field
in the newly opened quarter
of a year.

At the bottom of a meadow
the anger of America collects,
all its meanness and fear
swarmed over by horseflies
with maniacal wings.
I ask forgiveness of the raccoon
and the raccoon's god.
Then try to get some sleep.

Past midnight I wake
to hear small metallic bodies of insects
hurling themselves against the screens.
Again, crickets lift their voices—
lonely chieftains casting up
an almost audible cry
and shuffling their robes of dust.

THE CYNIC

He had never been good at it: the cutting remark,
mordant jokes, sarcasm that stings—

the whole bag of cynical tricks that can vex
like a swarm of vermin assailing

the listener. Hours as a child
he practiced behind his barn, hefting

a word, admiring its glint, testing its edge
on his careful tongue.

But he never acquired the knack of it. Nor could he
pretend to know despair

that rots the will, strips the mind
of its sanguine lies, the heart of its mealy visions.

He never understood those cold-blooded ones, true cynics
who command our greatest respect,

like presidents or generals or Olympic stars,
heroes of the two-edged sword

annointed at birth with the holy oil of vitriol.
And even later, as an adult,

whenever news was discussed, or the market,
or a nation's foreign policy,

he could never give up on the world,
never really fix in his mind

that image of civilization gone berserk,
a garden of poisonous clouds

blooming in the sky like oblivion's bouquet.
He remained an outcast, stunted

by hope. He would always be that boy in a barnyard
full of dumb, sacrificial beasts,

stuttering his cold and useless curse.

HUNGER

It was late. Near the end of the world.
Our parents told us: *Eat everything on your plate—*
kids in Europe are starving.
Their parents, of course, said the same:
kids in China are starving.
and their parents the same:
African children starve daily.
So hunger circled the globe, like Magellan,
looking for a new world of scurvy and rickets,
skeletons and hollow skulls.
We turned to fast food and pesticides, hormones
and hybrids, anything to fill the world
with plenty. We scraped our plates
like tanners scrape empty skins.
And guilt? Guilt is a bum half asleep,
half dead on the pavement
just around the corner from the fine restaurant
in which we dine.

MONEY AS WATER

"Cash flow" "liquid assests" "pooling our resources"—
it's clear that money falls from heaven,
drops in pennies, nickels, dimes, to gather
in the small depressions of our hands.
It's clear how profit swells and streams of money
merge, how waves of money move
through nations, cause a "rippling effect"
and soon recede. How some people
drown, while others stay afloat and keep their heads
above the flood. How banks are "bailed out"
like wounded ships and panic follows,
bubbles burst, small investors find it hard
to breathe. Its clear how money
passes through our hands like water,
and our sources, once dried up, leave us
thirsting after more. How funds
diverted, often vanish, and those without a "safety net"
go "belly up." How all we have
goes down the drain, and we get soaked.

THE CLUMSY CONTEST

He was good. Real good. Mama fed him
vinegar and nettles while Papa pulled his punches—
only inches from the boy's lips—to insure
a life of stumbling and dropping things.
So his hands hung helplessly
from his sides, swung with perilous
imprecision, like wrecking balls,
while his feet tangled and tugged in two directions
and the circuits of his mind sent up
showers of alarming sparks.
The secret of confusion?
To draw the mind in one direction, body
in another, like soldiers who defend themselves,
standing back-to-back, are lured
apart then slain separately from behind.
So when his parents read about
the contest—seven rounds with
the international champ of Russia—
they bundled him off in a warm coat
with their dreams: he would be
the one to bring confusion home—
Defender of Disorder,
Saint of the Scattered—such terms
to build his confidence and give him
heart. And it was no surprise
when he returned triumphant,
having floored the Russian with an incomparable
flurry of half steps and blunders,
a footloose bacchanal that left them hushed,
as if the boy were haunted.
And when, in later years,
his hands grew steady, legs
obeyed the simplest commands, no one

begrudged him that. No one
complained when his stammer vanished
or made an outcry when he died
one evening in his sleep.
But the nation mourned, wept for all
the bedlam he conceived.
Riots broke out, from coast to coast,
in honor of his passing.

FILM NOIR

An actor takes a job in which he plays two parts:
a cruel mafia boss who kills on impulse,
and a young detective out to save the world.
The story is shot in chunks, and out of sequence—
one day they film the young detective
getting shot, a bullet from the shadows
as he prowls a locked warehouse
brimming with stolen goods. Months later,
made up like the boss, they film him
peering through a window down his snubnosed gun.
When the film premiers, the actor
goes alone. He's never seen the movie whole,
not since they chopped the scenes up
and rearranged them. He takes a seat
and settles in, munching lazily on jellybeans
and popcorn. Near the middle of the film
the young detective breaks into a warehouse
and creeps among piles of stolen goods.
Suddenly the boss appears. His sullen face
fills the screen. He leers into the window,
pulls his gun, and squeezes off a shot—
the young detective grabs his chest
and falls down writhing. And so the actor watches
as he shoots himself in living color,
which causes him to grab his knees
and squeeze them so hard he yelps
and spills his popcorn. He charges up the aisle
and out into the street. Walking home,
he ponders his peculiar fate. The shadows of Freud
and Jung go with him, two thugs
that have followed him from the theater.
Who gets to see his own life rearranged and whole,

his self-destructiveness made plain?
"It's just like my mother said," he thinks,
"I'm my own worst enemy!" Not knowing
where he's headed now, or knowing all too well,
as he turns the corner into his new life.

CHANSON D'AMOUR

A cold café somewhere—Strega, gin…
In the distance: war. In the foreground: pain.
At least, that's what the protagonist's
face tells us. A portrait of intense thought,
as if pain were a meditation on the plight of man.

And here's a table. Here's a shotglass
and a rose. Now the soundtrack
fills the joint with enormous grief.
Shadows crowd the corners,
convocation of souls of lovers past
come to bear unbearable witness.
A single candle burns on the table,
covered with a scrap of linen.

                The war steps up;
the night sky flushes red; guns thud
and subside. He doesn't care,
the lover. What's death to one bereft?
Out there: nothing but rain; nothing
but mist across a ruined continent.

How lovely, the city, the trees—
black branches empty of leaves
perfectly congruent with his heart—
as if nothing ever again
will fill these avenues with song.
Nothing but the lover's eradicable luck:

unthinkable; preposterous; gone.

DACE

Junk fish, made of garbage and black silt,
mud given breath, if it were ever so,
I lay on my stomach beside the stream
and watched them glide in the current, then go

bounding like grasshoppers when the light changed,
casting lacy shadows on the bottom.
Fish common as dirt, big-lipped and hungry,
mouths made, like vacuum cleaners, to suck scum

from rocks and scour the sand clean. Sometimes
they'd roll their flanks up and their tiny scales
would catch the sun, throwing off a yellow
light, a dirty, magnified gold through curls

of water spreading easily across
the surface of a brook. We'd call them
Golden Shiners then and thought this dim flash
a signal, though for god knows what. They'd swim

in nervous, glittering schools, their red fins
folding and unfolding, translucent tail
sweeping one way, then the other, holding
them afloat. We'd use them for bait, impale

them underneath the dorsal fin, or stick
the hook from lip to lip locking their jaws
shut, free enough to wiggle there like sin
in the blue depths of a lake. And because

we were children, we thought nothing of death.
Certainly not these, plentiful and cheap.
We caught them by the hundreds in our traps
and always there were more, as if the deep

water bred them like grass or drops of rain,
not really singular, not selves like us,
but things to cast into the dark, countless
and expendable. And without remorse

the big fish, northern pike or bass, would sieze
them in a frenzy of greed, gluttony
that thrilled us, surged up our arms into hearts
that beat like pistons, mad with sympathy.

And all the time, beneath us in the weeds,
the mud gave up another host of dace,
black splinters of oblivion, without
regard, without an essence or a face.

RETURN OF THE PRODIGALS

Baby boomers, the largest single generation
in history, will begin to die in great numbers
during the first decades of the 21st Century.

How often have you made love to someone
because the Angel of Death passed by your door
throwing an icy shadow over your life—
just to let you know He's still there
in case you forgot, in case you thought
anything had changed in all these decimated centuries.

Something like that must have happened
way back then, while Hitler danced and Mussolini
grimaced for the camera. And even later,
after it was over and everyone breathed a sigh
of relief people went right on making love for awhile
and the babies kept coming and coming.

A great wave passed through the generations,
a tide of children washed up here
as if Life wanted to repopulate the world—
all those empty places at the table, all those families
shorn of parents or wiped out completely:
grandparents, aunts and uncles, even the dog.

But now it's time to call the children home.
Night's coming and shadows stretch
across the lawn as stars begin to appear
like purified souls in the blue anteroom
of evening. Death stands on tiptoe in His enormous
doorway whistling softly, as if to Himself.

And in Heaven it's quiet: a bunch of pale
administrators chewing the fat under a single
light bulb, the moon, making them drowsy,
filling in the hollows under their eyes
so you can see they haven't slept for ages.
A little bureau somewhere on the outskirts of Time.

So no one's alarmed when the first shy spirits
appear, almost transparent in the garish
light. No one even glances up when a few more
arrive awkwardly trying out their new
wings. They're no more bothersome
than a few spectral moths hovering about the room.

But soon an almost inaudible hum
starts up, then grows louder, like the approach
of locusts or an army of men whose feet
rustle on the pavement as they march to war.
Soon the room is swarming with souls
beating wildly about in their mortal confusion.

And you are there, too, as I am,
and your brother or sister, the first girl you ever
dated, the center on your high school
football team, your best friend—
all of us somewhere in that general tumult of souls
fresh out of the story of the world.

FROM *MORE THINGS IN HEAVEN AND EARTH* (2002)

FAMILY GODS

Rifling my parents' clothes for cash,
I came upon it one rainy morning
in the warrens of their closet
stuffed deep in a pocket of my father's coat.
Sex was secret in our house, nothing
to speak of in those lurid summers—
sweat made your shirt stick
and roads melted like spent tallow.
Father was away, a merchant sailor
bound for explicit ports of call.
Mother worked all day selling burgers
and antiques, sometimes a bottle
of cheap rum in the town's only emporium.
Now here I was, furtive thief
trying one pocket, then another,
until I plucked it out: more-than-life-sized
and obscenely veined. It was molded
of firm white rubber, a perfect phallus
in all detail—turgid, arched,
with broad shaft and hooded glans.
I held it like a person holds
a bomb—revolved it lightly in my palm
to see its other end—abrupt stump
detached from any body.
I stared until I felt it stir, as though
I'd found one of the family gods.
Then hurriedly stuffed it back
into his coat, more potent than money,
more explosive, and went on looking
for loose change. So heinous a crime,
so deeply buried in my brain
I might have made it up out of
sex-starved, adolescent fantasies —

though my hand still tingles and I'm antsy,
even now, speaking of it—
my parents, both dead,
might surprise me any minute,
punish me for announcing to the world
their secret and delicious love.

A FATHER'S JOKE

Hand in hand he took them to the subway,
his three lost children abandoned each year
when he sailed off, Captain of a merchant ship,
hurried them into the harrowing earth

below Manhattan where darkness echoed
and trains slithered up like serpents
to gobble hordes of passengers, then rattle off
scattering clouds of scorched air.

Inside the car, they'd sit beside him
swaying as the train lurched through tunnels
lit by flashing lights and bells
like funerals for the damned.

But soon he'd turn to face them, cold-eyed,
deep in his burlesque, forehead
furrowed with a question he proposed:
"Who are you?" he'd say. "I don't know *you!*"

Then he'd stare as though he meant it,
leaning back to register his scorn.
All their protestations got them nowhere
as the train plunged deeper

into blackness, picking up alarming speed.
"It's us," they'd bleat, "Daddy, it's us!"
"No," he'd say. "I don't know you," and he'd
turn away, composed as any stranger.

Once he even got up and, safe on sea legs,
wavered down the aisle to take
a seat and stare serenely out the window
as though he wasn't there.

On the edge of their terror, he'd relent,
come sit by them again and grin,
arm thrown carelessly around shoulders
still shuddering with fright.

Later, in the upper world of searing light,
he'd treat them to milkshakes, still laughing,
glad to be alive: a father once again,
Captain of their dark, adoring eyes.

SPREADING THE WORD

Knock-knock, it's the Jesuits next door
come to take possession of the books I offer,
a complete set of early church fathers:
Justin, Gregory, Augustine, Jerome.
They file in, all nods and smiles, white shirts and ties.
Each pair of open arms receives the Word,
stacked dozens high in heavy print,
arcana they can profit by. I don't confess
I never cracked the spines or searched these texts.
Instead, I lie: "I rarely use them."
But they are happy, hefting the inscrutable.
My shelves are empty now,
ready to receive the great poets:
Shakespeare, Homer, Hardy, Yeats.
But my neighbors, whom I rarely see:
I think them odd, a heady sect
disposed around a pile of holy books.
Yet, how must I appear to them,
enraptured by the works of Keats?
Each of us with heads bowed,
eyes fixed reverently on every word,
divided by a driveway and some trees.

WHITE, MIDDLE-CLASS, MALE

I'm tired of those lethal words that hiss:
Racist, capitalist, chauvinist, misogynist,
tired of constantly accusing myself—
though anyone is some of these, in part,
which simply living brings about.
Yet what if you could puncture a man
       and let the poison rush out:
Masochist, sadist, narcissist, opportunist.
       Soon, he'd be diminished.
His knees would buckle, his arms shrink:
Sentimentalist, moralist, romanticist, idealist.
       Purged of all those toxins,
he'd be like the witch in Oz
disappearing into a pile of laundry
—hedonist, sensualist, onanist, exhibitionist—
as if growth had been nothing but expanding hate
       and the body a blister of wickedness.

And when the hissing stopped,
he'd be a child again, pure ingot of virtue,
       model of original love.
But soon the world would coo:
       Pretty baby, pliant one.
And he'd reach out once more to take it in.

DEAR READER, I MEAN NO HARM

Dear Reader, I mean no harm
but someone's out for your blood.

Maybe it's personal, the friend
of a boyfriend of an ex-lover
who's heard what a dickhead you are
and means to settle things.

Maybe it's generic—zealots
from a neighboring tribe
who happen to think your God's
the reason for their suffering.

And what of pure chance,
the certified crazy with a gun
finding you among others
stampeding his rage.

Whatever the case: beware.

Someone's lying awake as you
read this, sharpening his knife,
dreaming of the sweet butter
your throat would make.

Someone's devising a small box,
touching one thin wire
to another, making the right con-
nections to unnerve you.

Eventually
Hate sits down, ready to lay
its scrupulous plans—
and your name's mentioned more than once.

This is not a theory.

MASSIVE

We love to say it: *massive,* to roll the word out
        like the stone rolled away from Christ's tomb,
                or a mushroom of fire claiming the entire sky:
massive: it has the look and feel of something
        substantial, something *ultra, deluxe,* or *super,*
                hence extraordinary, hence important:
He died of a massive heart attack, as if the heart
        were a third-world nation with a miniscule army
                overrun by a major power, its phalanxes of tanks,
its rumbling swarms of innumerable bombers.
        We never say, *He died of a little heart attack,*
                as if he had a cold, or some minor malady
that got out of hand—there's no such thing:
        when the heart dies it dies entire, the way
                a frown begins around the corners of a mouth
but quickly spreads until even the ears are involved,
        the eyes, the jaw, the whole face
                a predicate for the cool subject of disapproval.
Perhaps it's our irrepressible American spirit,
        the soul of P. T. Barnum invading our chests:
                heart attacks as huge as the Rockies or the heads
at Mount Rushmore, bigger than anyone else's.
        We stand there awed, the sound of the word
                still echoing around us like a shot that bounces
back and forth between buildings or hills,
        our own fate large enough to engulf a landscape.
                When have we responded so completely to a word?
And not a noble one—an abstract—but an adjective,
        a mere auxiliary, like a servant, when it's the noun,
                always the noun, the thing itself that kills us.

CENSUS

There are times I have to call them together:
all the people I am, or have been,
fetching them back from discarded phases
of my life. They come like family members
to a feast, not altogether willingly,
and take their places at the table in my head.
There's Bruno, the young tough,
fond of hunting, football and barroom brawls;
and Albert, the birdwatcher, with his
hip boots and notes. There's the pale sophisticate,
Harold, in his tux; and Frank, the intellectual,
with his sleeves rolled up. They come
from everywhere, like taxpayers to the block:
Jules, the actor; the rock star, Lex;
Benjamin, the traveler speaking seven tongues.
The room is getting crowded, but
still they come: Gavin, the lover; Louis,
the chef; and Sidney the author of immortal poems.
They pack together, like kids at a party.
And when I rise to address them,
they look so cooperative and meek,
so willing to give themselves up to the next
passion, the next life, they might be
converts of a new religion burning with zeal.
They don't know, even now, I betrayed them,
gave each a kiss and let them go—
though maybe it's they who betrayed me,
found wanting in the implacable purity of their eyes.

A NEW AGE

It was the heyday of vermin:
weasel for Police Chief, mouse for Mayor.
Pestilence reigned, and frenzy.
Then came the administration of cats,
followed by the rule of dogs.
By the time of monkeys, an afternoon dolor
gripped the city. Its denizens
lay about, picking lice off their genitals.
This was remedied by the advent
of humans. Now streets were cleaned,
feces piled up and dumped
beyond the city; all hair swept clean
from neglected streets.
It was the dawning of a new age!
Then came the reign of the lowly virus.

THE COMMITTEE TO UPGRADE CELESTIAL SIGNS

meets once a year

        to reevaluate old myths

            that spangle heaven:

       Taurus,   Draco,

    Perseus,

     Boötes…

    outdated in their Greek shining.

Quickly renamed,

      they are configured into modern shapes

        —cluster by cluster—

      Guitarus Major,   Double Arches,

   Empire State Building,

        Bottle of Coke….

Each fall,

     the firmament glitters like a new marquee,

     a hit parade of celebrities

        to correspond

   with the season's upcoming shows:

    where Cepheus glittered—

        the visage of an actress

          shines;

  Libra morphs into the body

      of a reigning hunk;

     the Pleiades burn all night—

        divas in a female rock group.

Trained over centuries

    to forget the pass

entire populations suffer

    from cultural

       amnesia

    catalyzed by constant change—

"This is NOW!"

                          a favorite bumper sticker shouts,

      and

                "Welcome to the Interactive Cosmos!"
Constellations rise and fall,

           brief as ads

                that flash across the blank screen

                    of heaven.
Computers work around the clock

            to thread stars

                  into relevant patterns

       while last year's icons

            fade

              like the memory

      of someone's face

           before cosmetic surgery.
At last

       the Committee votes on current choices,

              having sifted

      through a copious Printout

           of Possible Skies:
Hands go up around the table

              as they nod and smile—

      with the stroke of a finger

          the Zodiac is realigned
        against the infinite blackness behind the stars.

A '49 MERC

Someone dumped it here one night, locked
the wheels and watched it tumble into goldenrod and tansy,
ragweed grown over one door flung outward
in disgust. They did a good job, too: fenders split, windshield
veined with an intricate pattern of cracks
and fretwork. They felt, perhaps, a rare satisfaction
as the chassis crunched against rock and the rear window
buckled with its small view of the past. But the tires
are gone, and a shattered tail light shields a swarm
of hornets making a home of the wreckage. How much
is enough? Years add up, placing one small burden on another
until the back yaws, shoulders slump. Whoever it was
stood here as the hood plunged over and some branches snapped,
a smell of gasoline suffusing the air, reminding us
of the exact moment of capitulation when the life
we planned can no longer be pinpointed on any map
and the way we had of getting there knocks and rattles to a halt
above a dark ravine and we go off relieved—
no, happy to be rid of the weight of all that effort and desire.

HOW IT ARRIVES

The sun rolls slowly from one horizon to the next
the way a cue ball touched   just so
almost doesn't make its way across a table
while shadows seep from trees like tiny leaks.
It's the way the day goes: planetary, idle.
How water, in a clear jet, doesn't seem to tumble
and the sound of locusts chirring in leaves
seems something like a pulse   but whose?
It's how the evening holds itself in long abeyance,
how light reclines on stone and gravel.
How even the temperature is late to rise
and drags its feet like someone plodding stoutly
up a thousand narrow steps at dawn.
It's how the stars arrive, like early guests at empty
houses—shy, resplendent on the lawn.

MORE THINGS IN HEAVEN AND EARTH

I love that moment when Hamlet
turns to his friend, Horatio, and says:
There are more things in heaven and earth
Than are dreamt of in your philosophy,

meaning the ghost they've just seen
and by extension the harrowing details
of the spirit-world, which no one living
may know—but he also means the secret

murder of Hamlet Senior, which accounts
for the "earth" part of Hamlet's remark—
a whole spectrum of reality about which
we are ignorant as slugs. *O day and night,*

Horatio declaims, *this is wondrous strange,*
and that's the way I've always felt—
as though Hamlet wagged a finger right at me—
Thou witless oaf no wiser than a worm.

Yet it's not Prince Hamlet's quick rebuke
that rivets me, but the remark he makes
about the world: *There are more things*
in heaven and earth. The world's as various

as Horatio's response implies: stars revolve
and what we see is murder, infamy, disgrace—
enough to chill the blood and make our eyes
start out of our heads. But there's more

we cannot see, which might be beauty
or contentment, some unimagined grace
redeeming all that went before,
O heaven and earth, but this is wondrous strange!

FISHERMAN

A man spends his whole life fishing in himself
for something grand. It's like some lost lunker, big enough
to break all records. But he's only heard rumors, myths,
vague promises of wonder. He's only felt the shadow
of something enormous darken his life. Or has he?
Maybe it's the shadow of other fish, greater than his,
the shadow of other men's souls passing over him.
Each day he grabs his gear and makes his way
to the ocean. At least he's sure of that; or is he? Is it the ocean
or the little puddle of his tears? Is this his dinghy
or the frayed boards of his ego, scoured by a storm?
He shoves off, feeling the land fall away under his boots.
Soon he's drifting under clouds, wind whispering blandishments
in his ears. It could be today: the water heaves
and settles like a chest....He's not far out.
It's all so pleasant, so comforting—the sunlight,
the waves. He'll go back soon, thinking: "Maybe tonight."
Night with its concealments, its shadow masking all other shadows.
Night with its privacies, its alluringly distant stars.

AT THE RETIREMENT HOME FOR SLANG

they wander around in pajamas and robes—
unkempt, malodorous, muttering to themselves—
nametags askew on soiled flannel:
Zounds! Egads! and *Shucks!*
hardly revealing the power of their former lives.
And here in a corner sits *Balderdash!*
lost in a leather chair, his walrus mustache
breeding smoke and sputum and crumbs.
While outside, *Jiminy Crickets!* rests on the lawn
deciphering windrows of dead leaves.
But just a few miles away, near a small lake,
Camp Neologism echoes with shouts—
Far Out! and *Cool!* pick sides, as *Rad!* and *Gnarly!*
kick a hacky sack around and *Awesome!*
wanders in the woods discovering new fauna.
Whoa! and *Chill!* paddle a canoe,
shunning the rest, happy with their own devices.
Such gaiety is lost in summer air,
never finds its way across the lake as evening falls,
shrouding boats at their moorings.
Now *Tush! Tush!* whispers to himself
as *Hogwash!* is wheeled in leaving only *Jeepers!*
singing softly in fading light. But soon
even he falls silent, until silence itself resounds
more durable than any word.

THE GOOD DEVIL

He was bad at torture. Flubbed his first flaying.
Dropped his pointed trident
into a lake of oil and had to scorch himself
diving in to retrieve it. Came out looking
like a channel swimmer
sheathed in pitch. Once he stepped
on his own tail during a papal dis-
embowelment, dropped
the stomach of His Holiness
on the flagmarl where it rolled into a nearby
flue. They had to fetch it out
with iron ropes and sticks.
And once, while the other demons drew
and quartered—neatly
splitting a false prophet like a chicken—
he was busy gazing off,
admiring the tapestry of fire
that flickered on the horizon.
He missed the special Days of Profanity,
the Blasphemers' Sabbath,
the millennial Parade of Pagans.
And when that poet showed up—
the Florentine with sallow skin—he was off
gathering teeth in the Betrayer's Oven
to polish and string for his mother.
The Gossips assembled, glad for work, tongues
humming like locusts
during the first Pharonic plague.
Rumor stretched its four necks and rose on leathery wings.
When the order came up
from below, winding its way through the bowels
of authority to ordinary drudges like him,
he was banished and had to hand in

his pitchfork, tines unbloodied,
shaft still immaculate of martyrs' grease.
He had to slouch in utter shame
through the Gates of Perdition into a new
and chastening light to make his living
by the sweat of his labor—
a poor farmer now,
condemned to delve in wet earth like a simple worm.
And everything he touched throve.
Everything he planted grew
in prolific, earth-nurturing rows
glistening with everlasting life.

GULP!

a little fish
swallowed by a bigger fish,
who's swallowed by a bigger fish,
who's swallowed by an even bigger fish…

This could go on forever
because the universe is endless.

But what of its opposite:

big fish vomits up a smaller fish,
who vomits up a smaller fish,
who vomits up an even
smaller fish…

Until eventually, there's nothing.

Nothing out there; nothing in here.

But the fish swim left, the fish swim right—

nothing swallowing nothing.

BIOGRAPHY OF A MINOR BACTERIA

In the cradle of civilization: their cradle.

Kindergarten in the sewers of Rome.

Then across the Steppes on fleaback with Attila,

followed by ages of suppression while other nations raged:

Cholera, typhus, the black barbarians of the Plague.

Until the 19th century: heyday of Lord Frogbottom and Professor Fly.

And that was Eden: the fruit of every new cadaver.

Then the Angels of Innoculation!

Now they wait, broken in exile, for their Savior.

And He waits again for the right moment in their Kingdom.

Which will come.

CAPTAINS OF INDUSTRY

The cattle go on strike.
They want more for what they make—
each a bovine factory.

They list their worth, and nail it to the barnyard door:
Milk, cheese, hamburger, tripe,
And leather shoes for walking;
Convene at the barn at 5 o'clock
And let us do the talking!

The farmer demurs,
gloating by his fire.

In a week, the cows have eaten all their grain
and every piece of straw.
You can hear them bellowing at night,
like penitents in Hell.

The farmer's wife relents
and bursts into tears: O dears! O my dears!

But the farmer demurs,
gloating by his fire.

PRAYER FOR A TERMITE

Shield of Achilles, in which our Fates are figured,

Gauntlet of the Gods thrown down,

Little battering ram at the gates of our cities:

Forgive us.

AGONISTES

Your suffering, my suffering.
Whose do you prefer, my friend?

You think we have it
over a slew of cows or suckling pigs?

Perhaps. It's better
not to ask the question.

Someone may hear you.
Someone may answer.

Better stand perfectly still
and let the night pass undisturbed.

Maybe it won't find you, down
on your knees

saying "There is no God,
There is no Savior."

DISTRACTION

Are you distracted, my friend?
Or bored?

Have you seen the corn rows
leaning in the sun?

The civilizations of corn—

A perfect meat
to match our hunger.

And what if the earth
converts itself into mass wine?

Have you grown this heart
for nothing but curses?

Look: the sun moves,
pushing its head
through a strawberry.

The wind licks everything clean.

EN PASSANT

What are oceans, but the mind altered.
The sifting of possibilities.

A man in my village cut off
his right hand so he could think clearly.

Poor trash: his wife
sewed it back on by morning.

Those who rise in the night
chase their own bodies forever:

we sleep footloose;
the city is packed with such shadows.

At the bottom of one ocean
a thought formed:

No one dreamed this thought;
no one considered it.

That didn't keep a dynasty
from being wrecked or a soul from burning.

THE PRIEST

All night, all night in the chapel
playing cards. The priest was lucky,
three hands out of four.
Sometimes he hides them
in his vestments. He thinks I don't see.
He's like a child at a circus:
the bearded girl is just a bearded girl;
the dog boy is really a dog.
What a joke! And the others
in this village, what do they dream
each Sunday when he
swings his censer over their heads?
That heaven weeps for them?
What do they hear in his incantations
but the sound of cards
slapping the altar, one by one—
life from one sleeve, death from the other?

PRAYER

Let my body be broken
that it may bring forth a body

Let the sun touch my gravestone
like a brother

FROM *FUTURE SHIP* (2007)

FUTURE SHIP

The deeper we move into the future, the more we disappear into the past,
       that ghost ship
manned by family and friends, whole neighborhoods, villages,
       vast cities
or hunks of them like waxen combs broken off and taken in, their human cargo
       thriving,
who inhabit now the body's cells, its nerveways and staterooms, open decks,
       catwalks,
a grand ballroom filled with light slipping softly past the farthest capes.

    *

Blink the face of Jack Harrington, lean, moronic, eight years old, leers at me,
       wiry hair,
loud hoarse voice—like someone accustomed to yelling—his flesh already pitted,
       already old,
dressed in bargain-basement rags, chicken-breasted torso splayed with ribs.
       Blink
Nancy Bergen, pale face sown with freckles, green eyes, red hair swept backward
       in a ponytail
blooms in frosty light, as her breath bloomed, once, in the scintillant air of morning.

    *

The way out is the way in, as if the whole project of living were to gather light
       that leaps
off the surface of the world to scorch its image on the soul—
       that cave
we crawl into after millennia, inscribed with all we've ever witnessed,
       all we've known.
Blink again, the solemn face of a teacher hovers over my desk where I labor
       sweating answers
on the thin blue staves of a test book open to a blank page in nineteen fifty nine.

    *

Is it true that we remember everything that ever happened to us—every gesture,
       every act,
each person and the words they spoke, the landscape of a certain country,
       or a state,
how our bodies felt when we were twelve? That summer I fell in love
       and my limbs
glowed. One morning I woke in snow and the world seemed dirty and closed,
       a secret
I might never crack. Is it true the mind is endless, a lifetime lodged forever in its folds?

    *

Someone's weeping in the middle of the night. The light's on. I rouse myself from sleep
       to find my mother
sitting on a chair inside my room. Her sister's dead, lost in a car crash at the other end
       of the country.
The call came in, incomprehensible, late. *Go back to sleep,* she says, and I do.
       But not before
a woman I hardly knew enters my head, lies with me an hour in the dark,
       becomes part of my life
at the end of hers. I feel her stretch and settle in, bury herself in the dark continent of my brain.

    *

Stand on this cape—it's the last one, the one that juts out into fathomless night.
       Out there
a life passes, smoothly cleaving waves, all its gangways blazing.
       The dead
fill every window, and the not-forgotten throng high decks, immutable, waving their arms.
       Blink
there's Gary Woodman, still coughing, lungs withered by a childhood disease.
       Blink,
Mandy Strawbridge bares her teeth, skin so luminous and perfect she can never die.

GRANDMA'S RYE

Each day at five she'd
yell: *Get me some rye!*
And I'd scramble
to the basement where
she stowed a case
of Rockin' Horse or
Tennessee Stud, grab
a bottle from the shelf above
the bench where dusty
cans of tunafish and soup lay
strewn, unopened even
by spiders or the mouse who
lay dainty scat along
the windowsill, glass so
grimy, so close to ground
only the sickliest light
could filter through—*and don't
forget the ginger!*—quart
bottles stacked like precious
wine, I'd scuttle up
again and fix her drink, right
there in the kitchen, then
serve her in the parlor where
she sat collapsed between
the arms of a huge
chair, and as she drank
she'd stare at bric-a-brac
along the mantel, her
prize collection of poodles,
dogs of every shape
and size, glazed and fired
to a gloss in honor
of her own dogs, two whelps

with ribbons on their
necks, dressed up like ladies
on parade, she'd hold
their snouts, sing a little
broken snatch of song,
look them fiercely in the eyes.

THE FREEDOM OF ESCAPED BLOOD

All I knew of Europe was a farm somewhere
in upstate New York near Saratoga, a little place
my uncle owned, an immigrant—someone
from my mother's side of the family,
fleeing the Nazis in Austria. He worked
for a big American oil company, the one
with a galloping red Pegasus, emblem
of winged transit, freedom of escaped blood.
A big guy with a toothy grin, he loved
to laugh, face flushed, eyes dull with fatigue,
skin already wizened, as if old, battered
from a boyhood spent herding cows.
And his wife, my aunt, would stand dead center
in her garden, arms chapped, hands
caked with clay, to squint against the hard light
flooding her rows—dusty spheres of lettuce,
rhubarb stretching waxy, pink necks;
pebbled sacks of cucumbers lolling in shade.
They spoke in phlegmy, throat-rattling
German, orders or endearments, I couldn't tell,
though it's clear they loved each other,
shared the rural pleasures of their farm—
dirt-daubed, remote, a single country lane
lost among maples and stone walls.
You'd think they were hiding, tucked away
like that. But my uncle must have driven
to his job—a little warehouse in the village
branded with the symbol of a red horse.
One time, he played a game with me.
While he sat sprawled in a wooden chair
behind the house, I fired arrows into the air
above his head—straight as I could—
so they'd fall around him, coming closer

with each shot. I was aghast, but he just laughed
and urged me on, taking pleasure
in my fear and the narrow margin
of his escapes. But that was years ago.
Their world has vanished, sylvan acres
gobbled up—all that sauerkraut and wurst,
pickled onions packed in crocks, clean
slices of potato steeped in brine.
You don't see that red horse
much anymore. The sky's clear over Europe.
No bright warheads puncturing peace,
no more flames that leapt a continent
as though on wings, hooved and jubilant,
spreading everywhere, then out.

THE SITTERS

Do you remember Aunt Lizzie (very
fat) and Uncle Will (big dent in his
forehead) who came to our house
and cheered for the wrestlers—
wide eyed and raunchy, that tag
team slapping one another
with childish zeal, plastered
in their seats each week before
the television to applaud The Strangler
and Gorgeous George. Our parents
hired them as baby sitters,
specious "aunt" and "uncle," no more
family than the butcher with
his chicken guts and hocks; but
down-to-earth and honest. God
bless them, furious and flushed
with blood, Will's big hand wrapped
around a beer can, Lizzie's lust
as naked giants lumbered in a ring.
God bless their potent rage as bodies
hurtled into ropes, slingshot themselves
across the ring, and Uncle Will
wolfed down another pound of cold
cuts, lips flecked with spittle,
eyes bulging like a bull in pain.
Bless their pleasure at the Crusher
and the Full Nelson, their mawkish
joy when evil battled good and evil
lost, a simple fable of salvation. For God
has found them, sister, unannounced,
and wrenched their bodies from
their souls. And He has thrown them

for a loop, knocked the breath
out of their lungs, left them flattened
                              and amazed.

WHAT POEMS SAY

All poems say one thing: *death is coming.*
Why else do they spruce you up,
pale disheveled corpse—wizened, shy?

Why lipstick, rouge, a brand new suit?
We comb lifeless hair. Shut dark, inquisitive eyes.
Death is coming: like a lover, a corporate boss.

We have to look good, like someone on a dock
in his best clothes. Departure is formal. All poems know this,
and say one thing. Ransack your wardrobe! Straighten

your tie! What else is there to say? Others on the dock
whisper, a sound of water slopping up against a huge ship.
Now it blasts its one note: throbbing like an organ.

Seagulls cry, fly about like handkerchiefs in a stiff wind.
All poems say the same thing: *kiss your loved ones; say goodbye.*

TOWN BEACH

Summers we'd gather at the lake, whooping, obscene, to shuck
        our clothes
and don trunks, secretly assessing each another—who'd grown bigger,
        whose muscles bulged
with definition of a pecking order only we respected.
        We'd sit together
on the dock to smoke and swear, scrutinizing others stretched on towels
        or cavorting in the sun.
Little voyeurs, little spies—insatiable, obsessed—ogling women
        in brief suits,
almost dumbstruck with our own loneliness, our own introverted desire.
        Which is where I was
when Carol Cushman arrived, on the dock, having dog-paddled about
        then changed back
into my clothes, hair slicked up in a careful pompadour.
        Carol Cushman,
a secret I'd been nursing, careful not to say her name in case it smote me
        like the 27,000 names
for God, so potent, so holy, it might fizzle me to ashes on the spot.
        So when I said
I wasn't done, that it was hot, and all I wanted was to swim again
        no one guessed.
No one breathed a word as I trudged back to the dressing room to yank on
        clammy trunks,
hands trembling, stomach flopping like a caught thing, the whole
        black litany
of love complaints that grips the body and blights the mind—heartstruck,
        dazed,
mumbling to myself—"my love has come, my love has come…"
        stumbling out
once more on shaky legs, humbled, down-in-the-mouth, ashamed. Jesus.

BLUEBIRDS

Forget allegory, this is a fact:
a pair of bluebirds nest each year
in the eaves of our house on Oak Ridge Road.
The male is a shocking electric blue
so you have to imagine something gaudy;
something heightened, even in nature.
Most of what we get around here
is dull, soot-soaked, dingy as old bread.
But not this fellow. He shows up
each spring with his mate.
She's muted, mostly gray, only
a thin veil of azure draped on her wings.
The two of them scope out the roof
like a pair of newlyweds, looking for a home.
For some reason the female
catches sight of our ficus
through the bathroom window.
Why not build a nest there,
in that warm palace of leaves,
and not outside in the dead limbs of an oak?
She assaults the window,
striking it again and again, flying
into her own desperate reflection.
I wouldn't call it the tree of Paradise,
but it looks pretty good to her. I wouldn't say
she was practical, or wise.
I'm only telling you this to let you know
what happens, sometimes,
in a world we often look down on.
And they're not fools. They know
what they want, gathering what they can
to fly into the face of their longing.

LOONEY

They called him a bad one
in the NFL. Drafted from the deep South,
bull-necked and proud, no one
could break the spirit of a good old boy.
Thighs and shoulders heavy
with farmwork, he wouldn't behave.
His teamates complained
how he argued, brawled, drank beer.
What (he wanted to know) did they want—
a few heads bashed in?
Some worthless yards of gussied-up
cow pasture? They traded
him from team to team—a huge problem
with talent. He wound up
in Baltimore. Baltimore!
The citified, aristocratic South,
almost Yankee. And there
on frigid afternoons he wore the defense
out grappling with muscle
and bad genes. Though nothing can top
the day—head down, legs pumping—
he ran right out of his shoes
heading for paydirt, left them empty
on the goaline. The announcer
went apeshit, "What a run! What a run!"
Schula thought he had him pegged,
until he slipped up, cold-
cocked someone in a crummy bar.
Then suddenly in mid-career
he faded out altogether, too wild
for a wild game. Now somewhere,
heavy with age, he'll be taking off
his shoes to sink into a chair

before a television set, shoulders fallen,
knees jelly, tired of slamming
headlong into open arms.

TATTOOED GIRLS

Daughter of Chaos, Daddy's Girl, The Devil's Bride. Charms
that slide easily off the tongue and onto the body like acid
kisses, blistering the skin. Indelible sentences, lifelong
brands, as though pristine flesh can't wait to corrupt itself

which it can't, but stands wide-eyed, flawless and imprintable.
How easily these young girls pledge allegiance to the darkness,
that lawless world of possession and brute force. It's who you
belong to that matters most, who claims your vagrant heart.

I know they mean no harm. It's fun to scribble curses on your
arms, sport those hexes. Being sexy is a challenge, the taint
of danger in a glance that lingers on those phrases. Boys
love girls whose bodies have been marked with cryptic signs.

But no one needs to bait disaster. Horror taps its foot, and scans
the crowd. Waits until the music whirls faster, spinning dancers
on the floor. Absurd to think one night Chaos or Daddy or the Devil
might step slyly from the laughter to take them at their word.

THE RACE

I remember once my father beat me
in a race. He wasn't a quick man,
an agile man. In fact, he was stocky
with bandy legs, slightly bowed,
a full stomach just beginning to swell.
He wasn't the kind of man you'd think
could run, a man more used to sitting
in his chair after dinner summer nights
in a sleeveless t-shirt, a man whose chin
was slipping towards double.
So when he stepped out of the garage
that morning and said, "Come on.
Let's race." I wasn't sure what he meant.
We'd been cleaning out some junk
my mother wanted gone, old boxes
and a table with a broken leg.
We stacked some lumber in a different
place, and hung a bucksaw from the rafters.
"Come on," he said, and placed one foot
before the other, like a sprinter
ready to explode from his mark.
I think we may have had a conversation,
some words in which I indicated
how I felt about his body. Perhaps
I laughed at the way he bent down
to heft a plank, or how he tried to reach
a can of paint above us on a shelf.
I don't know. So much of what we said
is lost, as if we'd never said it. Now
he stood before me smiling, legs tensed,
arms at the ready as I lined up
next to him, sure I'd win. I was
12 or 13, my body exploding

with energy and new strength, the way
you feel at that age you can leap
into the air and fly. So when he
counted down the seconds I was thinking
how I'd laugh and taunt him later—
when he burst forth, legs pumping,
arms like pistons, fists clenched,
until I had to stop, not twenty yards
into the race, and watch him disappearing
down the road. How much we take
for granted, how quickly it's gone.

I ONLY HAVE EYES FOR YOU

The sun has dropped below the opulent
blue ridges of the Berkshires toward which I drift,
one hand draped languidly over the wheel,
the other scouring the radio, focused
like a safe-cracker on the dial, that hair-
turn to the right or left that might appease
the static, lock strands of tangled airwaves
into a pattern for a moment till they snap
into place, emanating as pure song
                                which is what
happens now, the Flamingos and their sidemen
filling the car with soft chords, a sound
that seems to permeate all space, resonates
even in my chest, as though it too
were a hollow instrument, made of vibrant
polished wood,
                  and now their voices
enter, pulsing together with tremulous longing,
Choo bop choo bop / Choo bop choo bop
a husky, harmonic confection through which I float,
and whatever anxieties beset me move off
at a distance like the dark, ambiguous hills
that recede as I approach—certain I'll be loved,
almost giddy with the surety of it, as if only
that will pacify the chaos in my head
until I have time to make sense of it all—
such sweet, momentary salvation
while the music deepens and a few stars shudder
like the prelude to a perfect night.

ROAD REPORT

Driving west through sandstone's
red arenas, a rodeo of slow erosion
cleaves these plains, these ravaged cliffs.
This is cowboy country. Desolate. Dull. Except
on weekends, when cafés bloom like cactus
after drought. My rented Mustang bucks
the wind—I'm strapped up, wide-eyed,
busting speed with both heels, a sure grip
on the wheel. Black clouds maneuver
in the distance, but I don't care. Mileage
is my obsession. I'm always racing off,
passing through, as though the present
were a dying town I'd rather flee.
What matters is the future, its glittering
hotel. Clouds loom closer, big as Brahmas
in the heavy air. The radio crackles
like a shattered rib. I'm in the chute.
I check the gas and set my jaw. I'm almost there.

ROCKET 88

We're all there, gathered
in the yard to see the brand new Olds
my father bought straight
off the showroom floor. Our smiles
flicker in chrome, stretch
sideways on the bumper to express
our joy. The women too crowd
close, sniff plush leather seats,
run fingers over plastic trays
and handles to exclaim, *It's so beautiful!*
while neighbors crush to ogle
tinted glass, sporty visor
beetle-browed across the windshield.
It's another age, one in which
an acquisition—dryer, t.v., Frigidaire—
brings people running, struck
with post-war glut, still hungry
from the long Depression.
We shuffle up to fondle tires, pop
the trunk and wiggle in,
then skid across upholstery
on our buttocks. It seems we're rich,
my parents happy, still young.
It's summer. Voices filter
through our trellis, mowers
drone as light rebounds across the hood.
When the others leave,
I slither up behind
the wheel, gaze into its bright
transparent hub, wonder

at the blue metallic background
set with stars, Saturn
with its chrome rings shining.

Right there: I'm sitting right there.
In all these years, I haven't moved.

GOODNIGHT, TEXAS

These fields belong to locusts—
not every seven years,
but every year. They cry out
in shrill voices,
and at night people
sleep in Childress or Clayton
or Goodnight, Texas.

I drive south from Denver
through a country of adobe houses
resting on sand like gutted boats.
At dawn, the crying pipes down.
By 8, oil derricks nod,
probe the outskirts of busted towns.

Through the Panhandle, cities thicken—
"Dan's Barbecue and Steaks…" "The Last Corral…."
How will you fit into this calcified earth,
this cowboy's dream of Heaven?

*

I won't pretend we were close.
I'm half astonished
that we've found each other
even now
on this cracked prairie near Fort Worth.

What a place to die.

Was it shame or fear
that bred our secrets, then hushed us
like that bead of spittle
soldering the lips of the newly dead?

Aren't you the point I once departed,
the blue wastage of my course?

*

You phoned once
from somewhere past Gibraltar, somewhere
in the heart of the Atlantic,
your voice scratchy and small
surrounded by a vast silence.

Your body floats, then fractures: legs first,
then the eyes, torn by diabetes,
absent limbs contrived of plastic
to make you look good—one last time—
in a blue suit.

*

Look, I've come this far to say hello.
It's noon. The sun rings off my hood
like a struck bell.
Somewhere your body waits,
almost virginal, whole.

Now the city hovers in the distance.
The land swelters,
scarred with wheelruts of old journeys.

Pray for me, my father, too.
We are far from home.

SERIOUS

Why can't I just be serious and stop screwing around, instead of making light
        of everything,
instead of always trying to find a way to subvert the moment, drain off my anxiety
        with a lame joke,
using humor as a shield, a deflating pin, or at the very least an obvious mask
        to hide my discomfort,
my uneasiness at the world's lethal certitudes, its cruelties and relentless pain?
        Instead I shrink,
as though suffering were a flame that might scorch me if I once reached out,
        a blistering drink
to someone sworn off drink for fear a single drop might send them hurtling to earth.

    *

At the most inopportune times—moments of tribulation or extreme grief,
        moments of horror,
grave emergencies, rituals and ceremonies meant to solemnize an hour, a life—
        something in me
disengages and floats free like one of those cinematic double exposures
        unseen by anyone
but the audience who after all is witnessing a tragedy, not living it, unlike the characters
        who writhe in anguish
at the fate that threatens to extinguish them while I look on, a bloodless ghost,
        disembodied,
untouchable, pallid voyeur safely adrift in the limbo of my own detachment.

    *

Humor a coping technique: like those endorphins that coat shredded nerves
        in crisis,
when the body knows the jig is finally up and nature provides this little dram of Lethe,
        a numbing draught

that calms the animal between the ogre's teeth—the "ogre" being death, of course,
          or pain so blinding
we could not endure it without anodynes or madness or the hand of some consoling god,
          some drug
that has a sense of purpose and infuses us with sudden peace, of pleasure almost,
          then shakes us free,
scoops out the soul to bear it unflinchingly aloft above the body's wreckage.

          *

I think of my forebears—Germans, Jews, Poles—all of them marching to camps,
          or in camps,
whittled to the bone by evil no compassionate mind can understand, lumps of meat
          caught-up
with rotten cloth, faces hollowed out by constant want beneath a gray umbrella of rain
          and ash;
I see them dancing in that sickened light, hands linked, feet flying, like lecherous serfs
          in Breughel
capering wildly in their winter scenes, trees around them black as clotted blood,
          hear them jabber
in strangled tongues jokes that kept them human in a place no unprotected heart survived.

          *

Once in Colorado on the steps of some crummy club, one of those rathskellers
          packed with smoke
and noise and unabashed desire, I sat half drunk, woozy, crushed by the weight
          of my own anguish,
my overall sense of isolation, a conviction of failure so pervasive and acute it caused
          a fissure
in the wall of self-pity, and through that crack I glimpsed the burden of human suffering
          beyond my own,

a misery grand enough to be called symphonic, or infinite, even cosmic if that word
          denotes
massive wretchedness, torment almost eternal, that can only be endured by God.

          *

That's when the endorphins kicked in to plaster over the little crack in my head,
          a tiny chink
that might have destroyed me—something in me lurched back from that precipitous edge
          to settle safely
once again in the familiar embrace of my own self-concern, something protective
          and alert,
source of my irrepressible foolishness, a folly so reflexive, so natural to my life
          you could call it
a trait, a genetic imperative, and the depth of its force, its spontaneous appearance
          whenever I'm threatened
might be used as a gauge, an unfailing measure of how very serious I really am.

DIABETES

I often wonder what my father thought about lying there hour after hour in his bed,
        blind,
both legs amputated, surprisingly gone. Already there were bruises on his arms,
        rotten spots
that presaged more corruption, small clouds scudding in at evening
        meaning
storm tomorrow, full-blown. He'd sometimes sung to me as a child: *red sky at night*
        sailor's delight
as if it explained anything, as if it were a charm against the real catastrophes of loss.

    *

Each public death is a secret death too, as though a person had to die twice: once
        outside
and once inside himself, dragging a lifetime down with him, an unknown world.
        It's possible
he had time to conjure it all up, set it in order, from the first flickering impressions
        of childhood
to immediate sounds—groans of other patients, voluble t.v.s, a clattering of plastic trays
        at lunch.
Or did he just drift, rummaging through his ghost chest, picking out one thing or another?

    *

I'm sure it's possible to have a hidden life, a life not even your family knows about,
        not even your wife,
though I don't mean anything salacious, some lurid episode that's easy enough
        to confess.
In fact, he told my sister that an early love of his had died, someone none of us
        had ever heard of.
I mean a life that's hidden even from the person living it. At least partially.
        Is that possible?
A life compacted of innumerable moments which no one can ever quite recollect again.

*

All I really know is that he lay there for months, maybe a year, his cataracted eyes
        veiled,
the smell of urine crawling in tubes. But if we have anything like a soul,
        it must be
a place inhabited by faces, a place of sounds and smells the body hoards up against…
        what?
And the earliest are often freshest, breasting time with an amazing ability to endure.
        Is that
what he was doing, turning back into carrion these memories could feed upon?

*

I remember thinking: *well that's done, that story's over* though I'm not sure
        what I meant.
I had the feeling it's a story we could never know, and that the grief we poured
        upon a father
touched a narrow part of what we buried, what we'd known. He lay in his coffin,
        lips sealed,
eyes sewn shut, and I placed my hand on his shoulder—he felt like someone
        stuffed
with old newspapers, the little anchors on his tie floating freely on a field of blue.

SAVED

Once I saved someone, actually saved a man's
      life, though it was nothing like the movies—
heart-stopping tension, imminent peril, body
      crashing through a holocaust of special effects.
I was out for a walk one morning in lung-burning
      cold when I heard a groan, and something
in me froze—steps away, slumped a man—cross-
      legged, a Buddha posed against naked brick.
It was early, perhaps 8 AM, too early for the stores,
      and I knew he'd been there all night
in his thin jacket fast asleep against the wall.
      When I approached, he raised his head
heavy as concrete, flesh gray, eyes frigid stars of snow,
      condensed and blank. *Stay there* I choked,
stupidly, and ran for help, my body skittish,
      racing out ahead of my will, or perhaps it was
my will that led my body, dragging it along the street.
      At the station, I delivered my report—breathless,
half in shock. I never saw the man again, but called
      to find out what became of him:
twenty more minutes, I was told, *and he'd be dead.*
      And so I saved someone, though "saved" is not
quite right with its freak bravado, and "assisted"
      is a weak word, too timid for the violence
of my flight. He's probably dead by now, anyone that
      careless, that drunk, and this is just a story,
though often I consider what he must have seen—
      another person hovering near, ashen figure
congealing out of nowhere, one ghost rescuing another.

8 MM

All over the country in closets,
basements, attics, tucked away in bottom
drawers, stowed in boxes under beds
in every household, every block, skin
cracked like old formica, eyes flawed,
liver-spotted hands bubbling like old film,
in every state, every town, reels
of family moments, graduations,
proms, sporting events, the baby
on his tricycle, the young bride,
mouth smeared with cake, the man
pitching horseshoes, sleeves
rolled, laughing, determined,
someone's father waving
from the curb, various cats and dogs,
the turkey dinner, the big
surprise when someone enters,
the shouting, all in silence, blurred
grainy hand-held figures bouncing
back and forth, focus waning,
the ray of light, like a spear, splitting
the frame, its tiny nova, cut
to Christmas, cut to beaches, cut to
puppies squirming under silver spray,
an old lady, blinking, confused,
the little girl on her lap luminous,
as if lit from within, a bed of flowers,
the wind, the snowman, the waves,
the whole parade with its tubas and
majorettes bugles and drums
rounds a corner of Main Street, the sudden
splice, and the darkness that comes.

A HILLSIDE IN MY YOUTH

Now the tough, slender boughs
of sumac whose poison
flowered in the sun, an oily red
that glistened on those leaves,
have grown back;
and the ground ivy
and the brambles rank with berries.

Now the golden stumps
that oozed a resin
dark as heartsblood, and hardened
into amber, have let
a few willowy branches out,
like gods who sprout
new bodies from dismembered trunks.

Now the underbrush, whose names
I never knew, uprooted
by my will or hacked back
into the ground,
have crept into the light once more
and stand woven together
against the old intrusion of my hand.

FROM SINCEREST FLATTERIES (2007)

OF KIM ADDONIZIO

We're all here at Frank's Place, lined up at the bar
or at tables, like kids in grade school, ready for a good
lesson, though Frank is fifty-three now, face
like a bad drawing, one of those wobbly portraits

kids scrawl because their hands shake, and Sally
blubbers in her goddamn beer because another man
dumped her and slammed the door, and Leon
thinks he's cute making his biceps dance with hula girls,

while over by the juke Teddy and Samantha whirl
as if love had a chance in this rat hole, this smoky basement
where each of us has been sent for screwing up,
for learning absolutely nothing in the whole demented world

but is Sally ever going to stop that dumb sobbing
because we're all tired, honey, we're all on our last legs,
so lay your head on the bar like a good girl and stop
that sniveling, put down your head and sleep.

OF JOHN BERRYMAN

Once down avenues volcanic with flame
we in our utter ignorance of time
crept youthful in love—much before sad fame
clutched me—proud in the body's extant prime.

O darling! than Aneas I was crueler,
sure, but not wise, immoderately dumb
as are unfledged boys about heart's desire,
so knew our beauty's worth not. I was numb.

Now I'd paddle through quagmires of hell
and before your little feet cast my soul
for one redeeming kiss, a smile. Well,
maybe God will vouchsafe me this last goal.

But time never dickers or reneges. No.
All's lost. Love whispers from its deathbed: Go…

OF LUCIE BROCK-BROIDO

Here in a blue bowl, the delicate light
of a Venetian hour, the ambient hues of narrowing.

When we toured the Doge's closets,
when we thumbed his cloisonné, my replete One,

what joy the harrowing marquetry of details,
Oh pity the dead their encumbrances!

Once, in a cold subaltern rain, the navy flocked
like patterns in a marble wall that alternate

as migraine stutters through the awful
cornice of a mind's embrasures. Yes. Just that. Just

before the hesitations of a wave's lip
murmuring its religious dicta, the anachronous putti

aswarm in their immaculate perspective,
hauled up in that heavenly blue baldachin of plaster.

O pity these confections, these astute everlasting.

OF STEPHEN DUNN

He never knew what people
thought of him, but he thought
little of it. Vanity was something

one could choose, like looking
in the mirror or not, a moment's
hesitation before stepping

out into the street where others,
just as anonymous, pretended
not to see him, not to notice

a man so self-absorbed as them.
And if he thought of others,
it was simply to avoid their questions

which were, after all, a way
of avoiding answers that no one,
least of all him, wanted

to confront. No, perhaps
the greatest vanity was anonymity,
a shrinking back from the lip

of actual knowledge. Not
the self-knowledge of a mirror
and the mirror's indifference,

but the self-knowledge of others'
indifference, which was always
greater and, somehow, more true.

OF CAROLYN FORCHÉ

We were born cursed by the desolate light of the Crimea.

Outside, night fields smoldered as the train switched tracks.
Somewhere near the border the guards turned away.

Il n'y a ni refuge, ni source pour cet ennui.

Twenty years ago gypsies hauled mandolins
across the *Tuileries* like gaunt birds,
their campfires flaring among tourists and cathedrals.

Those bells were not for us.
We ate the ashes of victory, the bread of defeat.

Your father was a ghost I kissed once
in the *Allée du Chat-qui-Perche* in honor of Francis Carco.

That was before these betrayals, the hospital
reeking of camphor and the nurses floating in their shoes
as if they weren't alive, weren't really there.

And whether we woke or slumbered, the hours
lined up against the wall, dawn wore a blindfold of smoke.

All men tremble in the harbor of their exile.

OF ALLEN GINSBERG

O, Allen, thou should'st be living at this hour!
    America hath need of thee! With thy Poesy
    oppositional to greed, war, fell corruption,
    corporate scandal, thy rod and thy staff…
    O Allen, we have need of thee!

Come with yr blood beard, yr Reality Suitcases,
    finger wagging at Power, bald pate gleaming
    in agony of wrong, dark Hebraic eyes glowing
    with Righteousness, clad in American flag
    for camera pops & celebrity-cam footage!

Come as naked eternal dark Angel among Blakean
    footlights! Grim as Isaiah! Glad as Marx! Come
    with yr Sutras of Sodom! Yr dithyrambs of homoerotic
    delight! Come as Moloch-Buster! Military-Industrial
    Scourge! Rabbinical Detective! Beatific Bully! Come
    with your scant Harmonium chanting Light!

Come as Adonis! Sad Apollonian Tyger Hero! Divinity
    of infinite brick smokestack Hades backyard gloom
    days! Cock-in-hand Monarch Madman Cleric
    of prophetic Dawns! Cowboy Kali! Old Soothsayer
    in soup kitchen tincan back alley Passaic red scare
    commie smoke room meetings! Time's Organ Grinder!

    O Allen, we have need of thee!

OF TED KOOSER

Let's go back to that lake
and rent a boat—an old one
so bleached and battered
you can't tell what color it is.

One that has drifted many years
like a dry leaf, while the moon
dove into the hills and stars
flashed like minnows in the sky.

Another season
and the caulking will give out,
a plank will split, the lake
will enter by the tiniest breach.

As lightly as I can, I step
into the boat—then row it, almost
too slowly to be noticed, deep
into the weedy heart of summer.

OF THOMAS LUX

Snakehead, Lamprey, Piranha, shark—
aquatic wimps compared to Asian Carp,
a.k.a "River Rabbits"
for the way they breed.
Smuggled here to suck up algae,
slimy vacuums, eating 5 times their weight
each day, gluttons of the fish world.
Look how they hurl themselves out of the river,
caused (some scientists think) by motor hum,
an outboard's drone triggers
something in their puny brains
and drives them wacky.
How they got into the Mississippi
no one knows. Then up river like a virus
in a muddy vein, state by state, until
they shimmied to the threshold of the Great Lakes.
"Sounds funny," says one fisherman,
"But this is no joke," speaking from a passing boat,
huge carp leaping in the air behind him.
What they eat: plankton, weeds
which native species eat as well,
(hence supply problems, hence competition).
Why we should worry: they leap as high
as 20 feet, break noses, injure necks.
5 species! Filter-feeders straight from China
eating their way into the New World.

OF SHARON OLDS

When the stranger came to town, so handsome
in his white shroud, all the girls went crazy,
shuffled and nudged down the long, slick corridors
to that vast auditorium to see who he would choose.
He chose me, mother, found me out in your scarlet chamber,
left me sweetly on its doorstep and slunk away,
inchwormed himself into oblivion, his birth-work done.
That was the public part. Later in the closets
and alcoves, the back-warrens of the flesh,
no one was there to witness the marriage of spirit and marrow,
the holy ghost, black as a shadow in his new tux,
the body in its caul of matter. Now it was only I
who nudged and shuffled, head battering the doors
of your arched pelvis like a supplicant
at the portals of a huge cathedral, wild to be wanted,
to be taken up at once and admitted.
And mother, you did—you opened your legs
like twin stanchions, wide on their greased pivots
to welcome me.

OF CHARLES SIMIC

The place is a mess, full of old
steamer trunks and mouse droppings—
a blind man's cane, a deaf girl's dress,
some rubble from a street in Belgrade in 1944
that fits together like a huge puzzle,
though no one's taken the trouble to reassemble it.

And here's a tailor's dummy, looking cutesy
in a dress from Paris. Over there
beyond the cripple with his lame dog
some shards from a once busy crystal ball.
Awe, Beauty, Eternity—stacked along walls
like so many art posters, yellow with age.

We might be on a bombed-out street:
flyblown windows of shops,
dark interiors where no one hides;
but you can see the butcher's smock
tossed over a chair, a stuffed animal or two,
dust settling on their glass eyes.

And in a special nook, way in the back
beyond the gravestones and stopped clocks,
a swirl of smoke which an old man guards,
the buttons of his uniform jerked open
while he sleeps, making faint noises
as though someone were still breathing.

OF GERALD STERN

And I have a right to say anything, even if
the cars go by, and the filthy pigeons parade
along the cornices of the old Pierce building
on 4th Street, insane with rage in the early
spring wind, lined up like bankers at a vault,
the coffee merchants and the bagelries,
the first tulips washing their faces in a gritty
light, a few bums rolled up in the alleys,
because that's what we called them: bums
and not homeless, because in America then
anyone who wanted a job could have one
and no one had to parade around in their rags,
lifting those pitiful cups, that sour wine,
no one had to wash his face in filth or shiver
in the damp steam, because you only had
to roll up your sleeves, you only had to ask
for bread, you only had to knock and someone
would answer, someone would unclasp
the old doors in the icy wind and let you in.

OF JEAN VALENTINE

Sunlight on the page

"an arranged euphoria"

      and then the door

You were not among them
or even inside

but beyond this reading—in a strong light

      too strong to be revealed

and then the door again: closing

We only half noticed his approach, still fifty yards away, one of those self-
       mutterers set adrift
gabbling fiercely to some inward wound, unsteady in his lumbering progress
       down the sidewalk,
broad-shouldered, burly as a fullback, until he reached that invisible boundary
       of awareness
in which each of us, all of us, are sealed, that chrysalis of privacy spun of our
       inwardness and fear.
Then suddenly, inexplicably, he lunged at my friend and thrust his face into
       my friend's face,
"I'm a gangsta," he hissed. "I'm a fuckin' gangsta!" and we froze, all of us, my
       friend, his wife and I,
suspended in that latency of violence and death we cope with every day but
       try to sidestep,
try to placate with our silence, our polite submissiveness when threatened,
       though it follows us,
dogs us, until I half turned back, drawing his attention towards me. He wheeled
       to face me
so my friends were able to escape behind his back, slipping away deftly in that
       moment's distraction.
Then I backed off and he glowered at me as I retreated and then it was over,
       just like that,
and the three of us continued down the street without speaking, as though
       nothing had happened,
still cowed by our fear, but when we reached the corner we turned to each
       other to ask "Are you all right?"
solicitous, consoling, placing my hand on his shoulder, his arm around his wife,
       each of us
shaken, shamed, pulses slowing in the scrim of newly opened leaves, hanging
       on for dear life.

FROM *No Other Paradise* (2010)

MORTAL MESSAGE

I don't wish to talk about the weather
but have you noticed how it's everywhere   at all times

we think some mortal message will make us whole

just now   for instance   raindrops
strike my window   so that each drop shatters beautifully

leaving a trail of lesser drops   as though each drop
were composed of smaller drops   and inside them

smaller drops   and inside them   etcetera   until

only the *idea* of a drop is left   from which all drops proceed

now the rain has stopped   and the droplets on my window
shrink   as though the smaller something is

the quicker it can vanish   then collect itself in greater parts
to reappear again   and not be lost

facing death   we think   *I'll change my life*
as if the life we lived were not our life   and only death

could make us recollect the person we had meant to be

and what of those who've known us   aren't we dispersed
among their memories   each family member

or acquaintance carrying a fragment of the person we were
until they gather at our funeral

to amass again a single   multifarious portrait

and when they drift away once more   each to his own life
are we finally dissipated   finally gone

words are the tiniest bits of an idea that might cohere
into a thought   and thoughts are nothing the wind can't scatter

until they are everywhere   at all times
though if remembered   if lucid and coherent   beautiful

KNOWLEDGE AND IGNORANCE

A jet passes over   making the sound of a piece of chalk
grating against a blackboard

I know the ancient cliffs are made of skeletons
and that this is not a metaphor

one afternoon I lay on my belly in the grass beside a pool
and watched two trout circle each other warily

what we learn is inculcated   then wiped away

think of the bones of those prehistoric creatures
and the cliffs as drifted snow

think of the future knowledge contained in them

wind wipes the passage of the jet away
until the air is immaculate again   a blue amnesia

it is impossible   really   this effort
to induce the invisible into images

for the moment the invisible is seen it is no longer invisible

language circles itself   looking for a way out
a way of expressing what it can't

after the passing of a jet   silence can also be heard
that only the jet's passing makes evident

and knowledge stands forth out of ignorance
like a soft cliff   which the blue waves at its base eat away

PRIME TIME

When the face of the ex-general fills my screen
when he opens his mouth to speak

I think I hear Cerberus barking in hell

but in the daytime   it stares at me
like an amnesiac   as though nothing had happened

I'm not fooled   with the flick of a switch
I might view the games in ancient Rome

bring back the emperor rabid for blood

my father hides under a cabbage
while my mother signals from a passing bird

they want to save me   but it's too late

there are ten thousand channels   each of them
linked by satellite to Plato's cave

the television ponders its inner self
strapped to the wall like a prisoner to his chair

when I slap it around   it knows nothing

when I shut it down   its whole glare
shrinks to a tiny campfire in the enormous dark

CARNAL ECHO

That fall I watched her board the bus   not someone
I had known   but beauty's surrogate

before that   I sprawled on my towel   a fragment
of bleached wood   washed up on the sand

sunfish swerved   carving water into secret paths
its sunlit surface and interior gloom

each betrayal I grew fond of   reminded me
of the one before   as though I longed to get it right

their bodies flashed   here   then there   leaving
no impression in the pockets of the lake

sometimes   we substitute another face or body
for the one we love   a carnal echo

meanwhile   light scatters along the surface
luminous as oil   the person you love

might be the same person in many people

who then did you really love   you can love
more than one person   you can love

the way water both condenses and refracts light

I dove into that green seclusion   blood hissing
in my ears   another world beneath the one I knew

and what betrayals   either mine   or someone else's

the body doesn't choose   nor the mottled pickerel
gliding easily among the weeds

in the future we can't fathom   faces loom   one face
eclipsing then dissolving into another

the moon floats above our houses   then swims away

SOMEBODY ELSE

The rich pay good money for torn jeans   the poor
wrap themselves in what the rich cast off

I stand before a mirror   practicing my sneer
as hermaphroditic fish cruise the coast

an ex fascist goes under the knife   then dips
his fingertips into a dish of acid

the smiles of fashion models blaze from magazines

every body wants to become some body
other than the body it's become

I was nearly fourteen   and longed to be Elvis

my parents lounged around   watching *Queen for a Day*

a woman they knew swore that in another life
she dallied in the courts of Rome

that fascist   where is he now   and if he's anyone
he's someone you might chance to know

he might be grinning from the cover of a magazine

there are fish who transform their sex   as easily
as someone switches channels on t.v.

and there are things we can't reverse   or undo

like this dumb smile   put there by a boy
practiced in the art of self negation   so long ago

WHATEVER IT TAKES

A small dog   the size of a rabbit   yaps in the park

the warm spell continues   confounding all reports

when our tree fell   the birds who used it for a dormitory
flew about the yard   confused

the president makes a speech   in which there
are nine covert lies   and three apparent ones

because of what he says   some children still in the womb
will be born with bullets already searching for their heads

I go about my business   like anyone

once the heat passes   rain whips in   pelting the streets

I watch a rat exit from a sewer grate like a prisoner from his cell
then hobble down the street   bloated   despised

nobody's born with a soul   it takes a lifetime of effort

the weather comes and goes   one day the trees
give out an audible sigh and let go of their exhausted leaves

we keep our guns hidden until we need them

LIVING WITH THE NEWS

These pictures   what do they tell

the day is a widow   the morning an open grave

it's not my hand that strikes them down

while I eat   their heads grow thinner
while I sleep   they murder in their dreams

they swim before me like fish in a bowl

is the body really this translucent

a disconsolate woman clings to her child
small and shrunken as a fly

when I've had my fill   I rise from the table

she follows me from room to room with open eyes

SNAPSHOT

Ten men on a postcard   clinging to the cables
of Brooklyn Bridge   they look   *one can't help it*

like insects glued to the struts of some unspeakable web

some things will die with us   memories   words
almost everything will die with us unspoken

it's nearly gone   the sound of waves
pummeling the beach   a seagull's sharp demands

a hundred years   if we had them
won't matter   much less the years we've had

those men   suspended in air   dry leaves
caught in a fence before the wind hauls them away

what do they say   in their best suits
perched nonchalantly above the flames of the East River

what matters is that we have been here at all

waves heave up and burst in bright concussions of foam
seagulls weave above it   slandering

in the distance   flags of smoke that never touch land

why not speak of what we know
instead of dangling   always   above the ineffable

on the opposite side   no address   no message

so they say   but what does the wind say
after the men are gone   blowing through those empty cables

SECRETS

A dead deer by the side of the road
one leg cocked up   stiff as a broom handle

as though it died in mid-leap
halfway between this world and the next

the teacher sees it   worrying about history
and its grim progression

the businessman sees it   head full of annual reports
and the jagged lines of an EKG

my mother always said she had good legs
it was the one thing she was proud of

and I remember the hours I spent   bored
waiting for her in the car

the miles we drove without speaking

now the mayor passes   and it seems to him
like an arm raised in a final vote

the waitress sees it and feels a coldness in herself
certain that her life will be wasted

once my mother lifted her skirt to show us
a blue vein already threading its way to the surface

the heart's dark tributary   emerging

the mill workers see it   hands bleached with chemicals
heads humming like precise machines

the scholar   the fireman   the ex-con

we all know what's going to happen   its so plain
and yet we rush past

though I hate a moral   even if it's naked in a ditch

later   the minister sees it and thinks of his sermon
how Jesus might have been a deer

how the last light is beautiful   but somehow obscene
crawling down the length of that leg

a cockeyed rebuke to us all   hurrying home
in the gathering dusk

which isn't a symbol of death   or time
but the ordinary knowledge

that someday the body will lie open to the world
all its secrets revealed

RIVER

not the source   or the destination
not even the middle in its constant motion

and not without resistance   the river hurries
in its current   implacable sleeve of water

traveling at all points   where is it
and if nowhere   what is this flowing

not the sky   but the anchor of the sky
nor the bank   but the meaning of the bank

the river wanders   but is always here
its root a fissure in the earth

its fate to fall   and be gathered   and fall
its surface scaled viridian   its depth

a drag of old newsprint and erosion
the past accumulating towards the future

cross it   and the nations hold their breath
block it   and its power deepens

a thought of the river   is the river itself
its mind a sunfish   its heart a cloud

wildest when shallow   it grows by moving
unlike us   spawning life   and where

it meets with islands   yields   to reconverge
in self-healed folds   like flesh

an omnivore   it feeds by daylight
ophidian   it swallows whole   adding

the world's detritus to itself   heart of rubber
soul of tin   a scroll of metaphor

that also stinks   giving up rank mud
the bloated dead   in dusky pools of light

the river is a feeding trough   uncertain mirror
shattering walls   transplanting continents

grain by incremental grain   an eon's hourglass
of elemental silt that bends

serenely into ever-lowering night
we shall gather at the river when the world ends

NIHILIST

He felt good for nothing, a phrase
he particularly loved, as it reminded him
of childhood, those useless days
when such words echoed daily in his ears.

He was nothing's darling, nothing's boy—
nothing to be proud of, and good for it.
There was nothing he could do about it,
nothing he could think of.

So little to expect from nothing! But it's
better than something, which always vanishes
into nothing. Philosophers agree—
nothing is mighty, vaster than something.

And he was bound for it, good for it,
nothing's sweet precocious child.
He had never been good at anything,
except nothing. Nothing could take that

away from him. And nothing would.

ADDRESS TO MY MOTHER

All those secrets   what can they matter now

you stood up to praise your god   your watery voice
intoning hymns   already half gone

how we battled   how we loved

what is the body but a narrow path
a night transit between one world and the next

and who can give more   not the grave
with its anonymous kisses   nor the earth

its pale arms turning at last to implacable stone

THIS CITY

No one has any idea where the wires actually begin, or end.
Long ago the plans were lost, and now there is faith.

We build towers to grow old beneath,
a permanence to mock or comfort our fragility.

Bridges are really stitches, hung over the scars of streams.
As though the city might come apart, break up
and drift out to sea like cakes of ice in a sudden thaw.

And under the city, another city, a city of rock.
Broad streets laid out in the Permian age.
Monuments of moss, the statues of catastrophe.
Great tectonic shifts of reconstruction.

And above the city? The homeless lie on airshafts
stretched in light, their bodies no heavier
than poplar seeds clinging to bushes in the park.

But at night, it's a question of whether the windows
are more real than the buildings, or visa versa.
It's a question of whether the buildings are there at all.

IN PARADISE

There was death in Paradise.

Before Adam, before Eve or the snake's long, voluptuous
Address, death entered the leaf
Like a drug, stole into the veins of light,
Inhabited the small corridors of rain.

God put it there. It was His presence,
The lingering odor of His breath.

Of three birds, banished from the nest,
One lay quiet in the grass,
And the grass glistened, green as fire,
And the worm wove through the earth,
And the earth held its silence
While everything else was being born.

Death was God's other face,
His secret name, the way the angels
Called to Him through the golden aisles
Of the Garden.
            It was the light
Inside the light, which was a darkness
Scattered in the air, like pollen, like dust.
The creatures were made of it,
            it was what they were.

Of three birds, banished from the nest,
One lay quiet in the grass
While everything else was being born.

NO OTHER PARADISE

Pale dawn   then banks of cloud   shot with light

highway salted to a dry crust   the sun a white flame

but no ice   the river a broad   rippling scintillance

the skyline's jagged profit chart   we wake to our own reality

purely imagined   the ghost-life of money   war

history's fractured narrative   we had a paradise

it was around here somewhere   near blighted derricks

tankers   bloated with oil   on the far bank

more of the same   and where bridges stride

listlessly   above the waste   raw sky empty of wings

    *

standing here   in this city   this gray sprawling

dismasted island   made of baby carriages

and sunken rails   stink of scorched rubber   howl

of metal   Lucite   mortar   polymer   glass

horizon of stainless steel   chromium nickel towers

so high   they lean *in*   grid on grid   finials and brick

cladding   the vanished hulls   asphalt slips

once porcupined with spars   and under pavements

scooped   blasted interior of spongiform rock

city of tin cans   conurbation of exposed beams

men with lunch boxes   dining nonchalantly in air

lives teetering on pylons   and the sea's indulgence

    *

slurry on the river   a liquid gel   and in the park
pigeons huddle by a wall   heads stuffed back
into shoulders   like rolled socks   wind
veers down alleys and mews   hurdles buildings
spills into the city's mold   then hardens into towers
catwalks   parapets   buffeting the few
who scrabble home   or off to work   is it that difficult
to get from one place to the next   tall gusts
bludgeoning cornices   cabs   the decrepit façade
of *Deutsche Evangelisch Lutherische Est. 1859*
meanwhile   Miss Donna   "Mystical Astrologist"
deprived of customers   falls asleep over her cards

*

snow circles the pediments   handprint of a child
on Fourth Street   filled with rain   sign on a cellar door
jazz until down   but dig in one corner and turn up houses
old pastures   parading troops   riots   slums
no longer crowded   to know is to guess   age on age
everything streams past this palimpsest   this eviction
of ghosts   and by the frigid beltways   prow
nudges prow   avenues come apart   the past is spliced
onto the present   the future snaps like a cable
nidus of incalculable ambitions   necropolis of dreams
now sunlight breaks fully on these stone embrasures

*

no silence   but steady tumult   night or day
skirl of iron   blast of brakes   wrecking ball
and dredger   *listen*   someone's key rattles in a box
we were born here   passing through flesh
to become flesh   in the white rush of acetylene
the boom of freight   arriving in a bright arpeggio
of taxis   departing in the echo of announcements
I didn't do anything   he says   *I was half asleep*
then a gust of air   before the train arrives
bristling sound along the tracks   like hundreds
of tiny wires   shaken together   a secret scuttering
the bastard slipped out on me   doors close   everywhere
and in the freezing air   all that was never said
glitters louder than jackhammers   probing the street

    *

there's always someplace else to be but where we are
hurrying uptown   hurtling down   highways
stream like gunwales   leaving our old address
while buses   slick as carp   nose down avenues
helicopters hop from stalks of concrete   even the earth
trembles underfoot   shuddering with departure
sky-hung scaffolding sways   settles under booms
and steel nets   coming and going   there are clocks
everywhere   circling the day   whistles   bells
schedules   printed with the details of ephemera
a nickel glints on the sidewalk   pressed into stone

    *

pipes froze   windows cracked   it was that cold
laundry hung like sheets of metal on the line
later   soot   rain   the bald sun-scorched arcades
blood stopped in the arteries   the intricate veins
of the face   squalls   blizzards   a hundred winters
buried in the mind   *this isn't a city   it's the world*
built up   and demolished   icicled and white
someone skis down blanketed ravines   the abandoned
offices   exposed manholes breathing steam
and later   gelid bodies   brittle as petrified wood
appear like pharos   under elegant pyramids
makeshift ziggurats   a mummified doorman stamps
his feet   and takes a long-drawn   glittering breath

  *

praise the filth   the narrowing   sexual nights
history's pages   thumbed over and over in the street
young girls trudge past   gloved hands locked   laughter
spangling the air   then a child   dragging a sled
such storms rise out of the sea   to reclaim the town
dragging it under a powdery   white   iridescent foam
praise the cinder   the compact   scalloped slush
the incalculable waste   box   and melon rind
greasy axle and lug nut   the flyblown   busted armchair
in which no one sits but the bleak   fugitive sun
praise ashcan and coal chute   brackish gutter and cracked
pane   how the brand-new passes through the present
to the harrowing   unspeakable dump   *don't let go*
they giggle   turning the corner with linked arms
if you lose someone here   you may never see them again

  *

angle of earth   and our distance from the sun
all these lives pitched outward   man in a penthouse
woman in 14-c   *it was around here somewhere*
higher and higher   time leans *in*   brimming the dank
projects   the rich basilicas   someone's hat
blows off and rolls down the street   who isn't a city
a generation   who isn't a graveyard   the flaking
broken stones   MOSCOWITZ   O'MALLEY
POUDELLE   VAN DER SLUIJS   VOSZKA
CHORBAJIANI   SUDHOLM   NJOKU-OBI   ZENK
passing through flesh to become flesh   mothers
strolling under bare trees   fathers turning in the long fall

    *

one shop trembles like a wick   windows
spewing flame   houses in surrounding streets
shudder together like dry leaves
sirens and alarms   walls reflecting strobe light
smoke billows out and pours into the sky   smell
of the eternal   scrapbooks   photos   letters
files crammed with documents   words beginning
to erase themselves   the past   lifting up and thinning out
the future   vast and blue   swallowing it whole   then nothing
but the pungent odor of burnt wood   water   sealing us back in

    *

Miss Donna   wakes in snowlight   no one there
only her cat   chary and alert   as though something might
happen   some restless apparition   or voice   *listen*
across the water   cannons rumble   as a ship arrives
ensigns aloft   and near the slips   drunken song
anarchy of gulls   fish market   pig stall   the butcher's
litter   this island itself a ship   breasting time
she hears it in the silent rocking of the shop   and now
as the wind luffs   rattle of cartwheel   bottle chink
blade drawn slowly over stone   sound of a dog
from a different century   shadows of flakes   drifting
down the wall   the insubstantial dead   the multitude

*

if it's all glass   why can't we see through it
river to river   its febrile life exposed   tier on tier
into endless air   and when we come down
a little drink steadies us   anchors us again to the ground
whenever one of my friends succeeds   he says
a little something in me dies   ghost-life of numbers
all that abstraction   trapped in concrete   all
that sweat   that heartbreak   just as the hairs on the head
are numbered   the breaths we take   going up
we say   to spend our day   suspended   between
heaven   and earth   how the invisible   the bodiless
can crush us   story by story   floor by floor

*

four a.m.   the savage markets   aproned men
in boots   haul fresh meat   hooked aloft   packed
plucked bodies   skinned sinew and scraped bone
a carcass swings   hacked open   to a lattice of ribs
across town   catfish lie   composed in steel bins
near moist hake   plush with oil   and knots of octopus
glisten in aluminum tubs   nothing can appease
the city's appetites   its cold lockers swung wide
mounds of bread   like fresh graves   stacks of lettuce
squash   potatoes   leeks   trucks arriving with the first
antiseptic light   the hauler's hands   bloody
with their work   the very stones stained with it
until their hoses wash them clean   and the river
profaned with garbage   drags its filthy body towards the sea

    *

praise the sewers   the black   scabrous buildings
praise billboards   their ripped   illuminated smiles
light erupts   spills from the center like fire
a spectral phosphorescence   leaching the ravenous dark
windows appear   statues in the park grow pensive
trees nudge each other   the moon swings on its black cord
and on avenues   thick with lights   chic salons
ignite cheap   heraldic logos   the city flings its halo
into space   a bright   tentative exhalation above the roofs
the shivering   muffled night   scarred with stars

    *

a hesitation   a hush   the rush of traffic slows
Miss Donna lights a candle   and stares into her own palm
on the next block   St. Bosco's Elementary   spills
children into the street   their voices   punctuate the dusk
mothers stroll under bare trees   and fathers turn
as though they could hear something   a bell ringing
in the next century   the ghost-life of war   *if you lose*
someone now   you may never find them again
for a moment   walls tremble   leaning into each other
as what-has-been   leaches into what-will-come
and in a mailbox   somewhere   there's a letter
written with a firm hand   bearing news that will wreck a life
meanwhile   wrapped in blankets   a bum stops
at the corner   and squints at a billboard for Clancy's Whiskey
"a little taste of heaven"   to calculate the angle of earth
his exact distance from the sun   in the morning
he'll emerge from his ziggarut of boxes   bored stiff
and chastened   ready to assume the blessings of his new life

    *

O fish-flanked city   crux of origins   locus of souls
we wake to our own reality   *just now   and always again*
train wreck   widow's cry   the murderous indictment
banks of light-shot   ineffable turrets   rise   the tide whelms
and pivots   praise the hustle   the shuck and jive
praise the boulevard's riot of light   who knows his homeland
from these littered streets   *hold on to your wallet*
and don't look no one in the eye   now night lowers
its thickening grit   and incoming flights   beacon the sky
who can tell his life from this rabble of announcements
from Sin City   "Open for Lunch"   Kotz Bros. Welding
Raju & Sons 24-hour Tow   HairHealth Inc.   Nick's Locks
and Hindleman's Smoke Shop   from no other paradise   but here

FROM *TIME~BOUND* (2012)

THAT STREET

That street lined with poplars, elms and oaks,
shadow-webbed, star-ceilinged, wind-trafficked
by blowing snow—is it still there, its shimmering
pavements and empty lots, its hedged-in back
yards with their plastic pools, their toy balls
scattered near one-car paint-flaking garages?

And the sad, brown houses sinking into earth
with their many-peaked sun-crowned roofs,
windows from which tears and laughter,
bits of screams drifted out into slow moving dusks—
are they standing with their grim chimneys,
their coal bins and wide stoops like stone tongues?

And what about the lawns, squares of sparse grass
edging up through sand, acorn-drummed,
squirrel-haunted lawns where a boy's bicycle
lay abandoned, guarded by somnolent dogs
who barked their displeasure at each lone walker
whistling for night to come, come lie at his feet?

You can walk down that same street, right now,
but it's not that street. It still exists, but do you?
Even now it is within reach, there across the river,
though this sentence will never find it, these words
that wander blindly in their meanings looking
for its leaf-lined adjectives, its lost nouns of light.

PRESENT TENSE

The trick, say gurus, is to *stay in the present*
though even while saying it, the present flees.

Words disappear into past-time by the end
of the sentence which proposes to arrest it.

Time is money, we say, but it is also language.
Words take time and split it into separate realms.

The present seems the thinnest membrane
between past and future, the sliver of an instant

we pass through without ever being there.
Before, we say, and *after* and *now.*

But isn't that what childhood is all about,
a pre-verbal idyll without time

before the snake of language slithered in and hissed,
You are dying, you will die, you have died.

ABOUT TIME

Real time, prime time, quality time, face time—
aren't we just talking about life but parsing it
into separate orders of experience? But experience
of what: attention, existence, consciousness?

Isn't time like the wind—everywhere an agent,
but invisible, blowing leaves, knocking down houses,
shoving the sea from one continent to the next?

Time itself is a destroyer. But it's also a Creator.
Sounds crazy, but that's the real enigma of Time.

And where does time abide, where does it live:
in cuckoo clocks (19th century time), or wristwatches
(20th century time), or sundials (14th century time)?
And if time moves one way, why not another?
Can we travel back on it, as Speke and Burton
traveled up the Nile to reach its ultimate source?

Time funnels through an hour glass, though
it's only sand squeezing through a pinched spot,
and sand isn't time, though it takes ages to make,
the grist of innumerable smashed rocks.
                              Arguments
about Time tend to end this way—where they began.
Yet time is everything, even though it's nothing.

Though not for us. For us it is everything, my love.

STAG FILM

"Poontang!," someone yelped, but I thought, *beautiful*.
A dozen of us huddled in the dark
to jeer a woman luminescent as a ghost.
Our faces flickered in a shaft of light
the rickety projector branded on a wall.
We sat faithfully through each position
poised for the thrill of a final cum shot.

Each new angle drew a catcall from us
sparking hoots of adolescent laughter
that masked our nervousness. But no one left
or even budged from where we sat transfixed.
I mocked her with the rest, but secretly
feasted on her body, her flesh, her lips,
and each nipple, luscious as a cumquat.

FRIENDSHIP

First, we broke in. Then we broke every window
in the place. It was quick work, and we were well suited
for it, being young, and inconsolable, and angry.

Of course, the windows were symbolic, but what
did that matter? They broke as well one way
as another, shattering with an unconditional sound.

And who started it, him or me, made no difference
either. We were equal to the task, our bodies
not separate, but a pair of hands ready for the wrecking.

Then we fled, he to his gloating satisfaction, and I
to mine, though I soon began to understand
how actions cause equal and opposite reactions.

When the police arrived, my parents wondered
how I could have done it, hadn't they raised me
better than this, and wasn't I ashamed of myself now?

I was. Which is what led me to implicate him,
and claim he'd started it. In fact, that he had
done it all, and I'd only stood by watching, aghast.

The cop who took this statement eyed me coldly.
He knew better. And soon I broke down, sobbing,
ready to say anything, ready to tell him then

what I had no words to explain until now,
that betrayal is sometimes the greater part of friendship
and friendship's as fragile as glass, as easy to shatter.

GLOBAL WARMING

I've been wanting to write a poem about the icecaps,
wondering how to make myself care. It's so huge, this event, like God,
not really anywhere, yet everywhere at once, so hard to grasp
which is why the newspapers go on clucking about political correctness
while pundits let us know that the latest research indicates
the South Beach diet may not be that effective, or even good for us,
and human cloning may soon be a fact, but is it ethical and should we pursue it?

I remember once in Colorado, after a night of carousing, my friends
and I stumbled through town, arms linked, yelling at the top of our lungs:
"The icecaps are melllllting! The icecaps are melllllting!"
each of us a drunken Paul Revere, though we woke no one up,
not a window blazed in that sleeping village, and the next morning
frost spangled the meadows and blood pounded in our heads
the way people in cheap hotels pummel the walls, demanding quiet.

In my poem birds circle a dead seal on the ice, its blood leaking
out into the snow the way strawberries crushed against linen
spread from thread to thread until the original stain is ten times larger
than when it began and birds wheel above, shrieking, waiting for the body to bloat,
then burst, its hidden delicacies exposed until the bones,
clean and ribbed as ice, blend into the snowpack.

Every day, huge hunks split off and plunge into the sea, which has been filmed,
you can watch it on Discovery Channel between promos for "Living Predators
of the African Veldt" and "The Golden Treasures of Tutankhamun."
It's like watching the demolition of an enormous building
which will have catastrophic consequences for every creature on earth,
including micro-life—nits, mites, diatoms, bacilli—the chemical structure
of their tiny world shifting in a cataclysm of infinite degrees
but just enough to swathe them in a genocidal broth of heat and saline.

Still, the pretty young newswoman smiles as she assays the weather map:
"This has been the warmest winter on record," she purrs, making it sound
so reassuring, so fortunate. "Savor these days," she says, and laughs.
Such a gorgeous messenger—no demon or witch, no Sybil—
not even some awe-inspiring angel descending in a blast of light
to make its announcement.

                                But it's worse than nuclear war,
it's irreversible and planetary which is why the peak of Kilimanjaro is now mud,
and Venice takes another stride into the sea. Such a beautiful catastrophe, tipping towards
Eden, then farther, into the desert which in a hundred years will be almost everywhere
and whoever's left will be living at the poles about to vanish into light at the edge
of the horizon. Unfortunate explorers. Savor these incomparable days.

FOREST

No undergrowth   and the trees widely spaced   so to walk
in the forest is like walking through a public building

at least   one kind of forest   but there is another

empire of moss   kingdom of cambium and phloem

————————————

If the mind is known   a sunblown clearing in the trees
more is hidden   or is the mind itself a forest

an abstract tangle   clogged with shattered stumps and thorns

————————————

Heading up the mountain   I was less than Hansel
and more a swaggering naif   the only darkness

what the trees might scatter   stippling the path

dawn extruded dowels and golden planes of light   fans
of luminescence   thick with motes

————————————

Is it possible
to walk in one forest   without walking in the other

here and there   spines of boulders knuckle up
a stump narrates its memory of flame and drought

————————————

Trees are singular   yet can't be seen   only the woods
massing their fabric of leaves   only the fabric's tearing
and repair   the water's soft thread

———————— ————————

I'm looking for a door
that will allow me to enter the forest

leafmeal   pine duff   scurf of seasons

I know what I'm looking for   but I don't know where it is
or maybe I know where it is

but I don't know what I'm looking for

————————————————

To clear the forest will do no good

for what is left is its absence   and so the forest
re-asserts itself   its remembered paths

and coverts   thickets of memory in which we lose ourselves

————————————————

Whatever we have neglected or haven't done
that is the forest   so the woods are a kind of time   a clock
whose hands are foliage and rain   or is the forest
a cemetery   an overloaded ship   a smoky den

————————————————

Whatever it is or resembles   it's everywhere   like
a boy who leaves home to find out he's become someone else
a boy whose footsteps   whose memories   are bread

———————————————

Leaving the forest   we carry it with us
a spreading umbrage   growing vaster with years

it breaks   finally   out of us   overrunning the pales
the gardens   the manicured lawns   until

the edge of one forest touches the other   and that's
where it finally ends   and the real forest begins

A THOUSAND KIM

"Dutch Schultz's deathbed ravings covered a wide range—all the way
    from mysterious million-dollar deals to assorted pals
        and double-XX guys to Communists, of all things.
    One sentence confounded everybody, even
the poets: *A boy has never wept, nor dashed a thousand kim.*
    What did the dying badman mean?" Well, who knows.
        History may never repeat itself, but it stutters.
    Time machineguns events at us, and we stagger,
bleeding from the holes in our hearts. On television
    a veteran back from Iraq boasts, "I looked death in the eye.
        I fought with death and I won." He glares
    at the camera, minus two legs (below the knee), the left side
        of his face disfigured, a ruddy lump of scars.
"How many people can say that?" he asks. No one replies. His image
    fades, and a commercial for Ambien splashes onto the screen.

§

It's hard to rest these days. Nightmares gallop through our brains,
    lids jitter in REM sleep, even our legs lurch and need
        to be calmed. *Suffering and death are of little interest*
    to the artist, thought Gertrude Stein and as the Second
World War approached, remarked: "I could not see why there being
    so many more of them made it any more interesting."
        Well who knows. A hundred kim, or a thousand
    are hard to visualize. That's why the government hides the bodies
and lead still kills, leaching into the brain from the brightly painted surfaces
    of toys. "No world," said my friend, "could be stranger
        than this one!" and I was beginning to see what he meant.

§

What a poor tool our brains are for making sense of anything.
From the *Falx cerebri* down to the *Teritorium of Cerebellum,*
we're stymied, and a bullet doesn't help, or a fleck
of carcinogenic paint lodged neatly in the forebrain. Every time I pass
a child on the corner I think: "He could be packing a gun." Then I laugh
at my own foolishness. But last night in my sleep a child shot
another child, and I did nothing. I didn't even wake up
until a garbage truck slammed down our street and for some reason
I thought of Will Durant, the philosopher, who calculated that there have been
only twenty-nine years in all of human history during which
there was not a war underway somewhere.
Maybe we should wear seatbelts when we go to bed. Maybe
we should ban lead from the body altogether, so we never have to endure
the sight of a mutilated boy weeping.

§

If young minds soak up knowledge "like a sponge," age wrings
it all out again until compassion becomes bloodlust and history
is honed to a single point. Maybe that point,
smaller than a period, in which the universe was packed
before the Big Bang ripped it open and out sprang St. Francis and Jeffrey
Dahmer, Ghandi and Dutch Schultz, each animated by a kind
of brain. "Dinosaurs had two brains," my friend said, "for all
the good it did them—one in the head, and one in the tail." Scaly
hook-and-ladders negotiating pre-history's curves, though a comet
did them in, like a stray bullet wandering a neighborhood
until it found its random target, earth, which some
have likened to a massive brain with its folded mountains,
its bright ideas like evolution or volcanoes spewing lava into the sea.

§

After World War I the Surrealists wanted to go to sleep forever,
        and poor Appolinaire did, but not before a sliver of the real world
                pierced his skull and a crowd of citizens massed outside
        his window chanting *Guillaume! Guillaume!* like a mother
calling her child home at dusk, while the movies of George Méliès
        were melted down to make heels for soldiers' boots.
                This was no dream, but a bizarre variant of beating
        ploughshares into swords as the French army plodded off to war
shod in Méliès' films, winsome illusions of that inventive movie-house magician.
        Death longs to infiltrate the world and experience life, if only
                briefly, borrowing our bodies before turning back
        into its own emptiness. Just this morning, twelve-feet high on the side
of a bus, the picture of a man grinning warmly, with blood spattered
        forehead and cheeks, rolled past with the legend:
                "America's favorite serial killer" spelled out in red paint,
        a sentence that might confound anyone, while the rest of us
shopped for artichokes and bagels, cut-rate carpets and white wine.

§

The world offers up its runes, its daily figments of reality, though
        I don't mean to exclude myself in any of this, as no one is excluded,
                but dragged ineluctably into to a wide net
like that purse-seine Robinson Jeffers imagined, all of us victims
        of interdependence until "Now there is no escape. We have gathered
                vast populations incapable of free survival…each person himself
        helpless," and so on. A thousand kim, a million kim. Like this pale
boy swaggering past, in black denim trousers and t-shirt, chrome studs
        glittering in his ears and lips in self-crucifixion, Fuck You Very Much
                stenciled across his chest. The world to him is a madhouse,
        a threat to his existence. It's a no-brainer as far as he's
concerned. Wars and future wars: the same war burning from decade
        to decade, as a pile of leaves catches fire from leaf to leaf,
                or a forest from tree to tree. The same spark of anger from ten
        thousand years ago when Cain picked up that rock and brained his brother.

§

But no one can remember that far back. Memory contains its own
       erasure, each generation another chapter in history's
            long amnesia. When a politician on t.v. says "we're going
      to see that this never happens again," I laugh out loud,
though it gives me no pleasure. I think of all the "eternal flames"
      burning around the world, polished cenotaphs
         containing nothing but the memory of unknown
      soldiers, their limbs so scattered they couldn't gather them up
to give them a decent burial. "History teaches us…" he's now saying,
      the t.v. announcer, and I wonder what he'll say next?
        If Cain and Dutch Schultz were brothers,
      what can we expect from two pounds of marbled
gray matter Hippocrates first located as the source
      of the mind—though long before that the Greeks and Egyptians
thought the mind resided in the heart, which is far more desirable.

§

Memories are dreams from which we don't wake up, until they become
      so distant it's as if they don't matter at all, or somehow never existed.
        Is hope a recurrent dream from which we never
      wake? The other night my wife half-sat up in bed and said
very clearly, very firmly, "Time promise in paradise everything is well,"
      then fell asleep again, and I did too, hoping that dreams
        still have validity and forecast the future as they did for the Pharoahs
      who ignored them at their peril, or woke in celebration of the coming
harvest, or a daughter's impending wedding. Who knows. But this morning
      in front of me in line at the bank, I stared at a question mark
        tattooed on the back of a man's shaved head, there, at the base
      of his skull where his spinal cord met his brain, the curled
blue hook of ink floating over a point, no bigger than a period, out of which
      the universe might one day emerge, or into which
      it might just as suddenly again, and without reason, disappear.

TOMORROW AND TOMORROW

Of *course* there's an afterlife, and one
after that, and another, etc., until the afterlives
circle eternity to become the life
you lived before this one, making this one
an afterlife too. No wonder you sleep late,
trying to avoid the little tasks and obligations,
the aches and pains that make up yesterday's afterlife
which is, of course, today's present.
There's no avoiding that. Though your head
aches to think of it, and you'd rather
linger by the window with your coffee
watching the neighbor's dog chase its tail.
Still, you can't help thinking that maybe
the present is just a beach on which all our yesterdays
have washed up, hollow and resounding.
But resounding with what? This will get you
nowhere, you think, and go back
for another cup, though it occurs to you
that you've done this all before too—
not only the cup of coffee you just drank,
but all the coffees on all those other mornings…
Now you're back where you started,
and your head aches again, and you want
nothing but to sit there peacefully in the window
watching the neighbor's dog chase its tail
never really catching it, yet never giving up.

LOVE POEM

Once, my poor distracted wife
put her bra into the freezer, where I found it in the morning
stiff with frost. And once, she put rice
into the bottom of my cup of tea, mistaking it for sugar—
the rice, that is—thinking it would sweeten
the cloudy brown dregs, then handed it to me with a smile.
And once, wearing only her nightgown
and my laced-up hiking boots, she stepped daintily
out into the snow behind our house and waded
through three-foot drifts like a bride lifting the hem of her skirt—
a memory clearer to me than our own wedding.
Sometimes love is not that serious, and what we love
is joy and the love joy brings. Though even that
is too complicated for what I feel when I recall her
standing in her garden in muddy overalls,
hands encased in thick gloves, rubber boots
up to her knees, a trowel or mulching fork in one of her hands.
Because love isn't always formal, either,
decked out in evening gowns, carrying an expensive
handbag and wearing a string of pearls.
Mostly it's frowsy and real, red-faced and smacking
its lips in the morning, a thread of dried blood
where the razor with its one keen tooth bit into a delicate ankle.
Love is there every day, the smell of cooking
in its hair, lips chaffed in the first frost,
argumentative and cross, crying at nothing,
then laughing hysterically at its own joke, or yours
as it trudges through snow or fishes a bra out of the freezer
where it has hibernated overnight. Seriously.

FOR MIKLÓS RADNÓTI

May 5, 1909–November 9, 1944

You lie awake among the snores and groans,
the stifled cries that nightmares cause,
haunting the sleepers. Outside, fog settles
on the barracks like a blanket on a corpse.

Halfway across the world I'm awake too,
a child only six months old, whose mother
cups his head with a tender hand, to whom
she coos, then tucks him under soft covers.

By what light do you scratch a letter
to your wife—not just a letter but a poem
in which you tell her of your dreams, the dream
of every man there: "Ah, does *our* home

still exist…Is it still as when we left it?"
Perhaps the moon, sliced by sharp wires
spills into the cramped confines of your room,
spreading the hellish glint of pale fires.

Those scratchings in the dark have reached us here
Miklós, in the light of a future age
you never lived to see. And today it's me,
I'm the one who reads your poems, page by page,

and lives your nightmares with you, though
I never had to cower like a trapped
animal. We shared nothing but the fragment
of a year until fate found you and stopped

your words. But I'm alive to tell you
that your poems survive, your poems were saved
and are read, even in this alien tongue,
though you took them with you to your grave.

MELVILLE AT THE CUSTOM HOUSE

Every ship whose bow nudged this island
cursed you, cargoed with its distance,
exotic lands from which you once drew plots.
Those first two novels baited fame.
But no longer. Without your public
you were exiled sure as any outcast on his rock,
and that building was a rock, a headland
of indifference carved in marble.
The toll was severe. Drinking, rages, the critics'
savagery greater than any you had known.
Your wife screeched stories of abuse,
your children drifted off to separate deaths.
You trained weak eyes on pages wrought
with numbers enigmatic as Queequeg's tattoos.
Six days a week for nineteen years,
four bucks a day. It adds up. Back home at night,
you squinted at the lines of *Clarel,* that pilgrimage
in verse. God remained a phantom sail
on a lost horizon, something you could not believe
nor stop pursuing. At dawn, without fail,
you'd re-embark down Broadway towards the office
circled by the screams of brokers picking
at the carcass of the Stock Exchange.
You died in your own room, loved only
by Elizabeth, a few grandchildren disposed
around the bed. Never mind that stone
at Woodlawn with its empty scroll
far from Manhattan and the Custom House.
      That building was your tomb.

A MOMENT

I keep returning to that moment, one
day at your kitchen table with the sun
slanting in through the glass above your sink.
You stood before me, brushing your long hair,
stroke after stroke in the astonished air
while you talked of nothing, and I sipped my drink.

Then suddenly you bent your head, and threw
your hair forward in a bright fan to show
your beauty in a simple act, at once
casual and contrived, while I sat there
like some stone figure in a stone chair—
such blatant beauty required a response.

But I did nothing, though my heart halted
in my chest, a small, numb, exalted
animal, until you tossed that golden wrack
of hair to settle once again upon
your shoulders and you smiled your wan
smile and I recalled myself, and smiled back.

INSIDE JOB

We begin inside until we are outside
which is the other side of the story,
though we never forget that inside the beginning
is the ending, even if we cannot see it,
and inside the ending is the lost beginning,
the yin and yang of everything there is,
balanced on the fulcrum of our choice,
and inside choice is fate, while inside fate
is a road, long as your life, which choice
has imagined and fate will build
paving over the other choices we might have made
until it may seem that they never existed,
residual possibilities of a fossil life
which remains inside us the way the imprint
of an ancient fern remains inside the mud
that once enclosed it, baked into stone
by the early sun that spun wildly in the sky.

SOME LATE ADVENTURES WITH THE SOUL

I.

Some days, like today, my soul feels as young as an infant
taking its first sip of milk. The sky looks out from the photograph
of a sky framed on a wall in a room where people walk,
staring into the image of a sky. Outside, of course, the real sky
at which no one is looking for the moment. Across it,
the shadow of something running, as if the earth were burning,
casting an image upwards, and not the other way around.
Maybe it was the sun, wanting only to look up at itself,
wanting to see its own majesty for once, inconceivable, and at a distance.

II.

Clouds hide their ashen faces, and the river lurches between banks
describing its passage south in a blade of sunlight where whole forests
flourish, and die. Far away, under mountains, horses thrust their heads
into that moment of green fire and crickets sing *omni*
gloriosa omni blessing the dust, the wild fractures in the earth.
If I have a soul, it doesn't belong in a church, any more than the forest
which hesitates, each leaf cocked, listening. A man has come out
into his backyard to sit in his lawn chair, and look up,
the pith of his brain greater than anything he can see, and everything beyond.

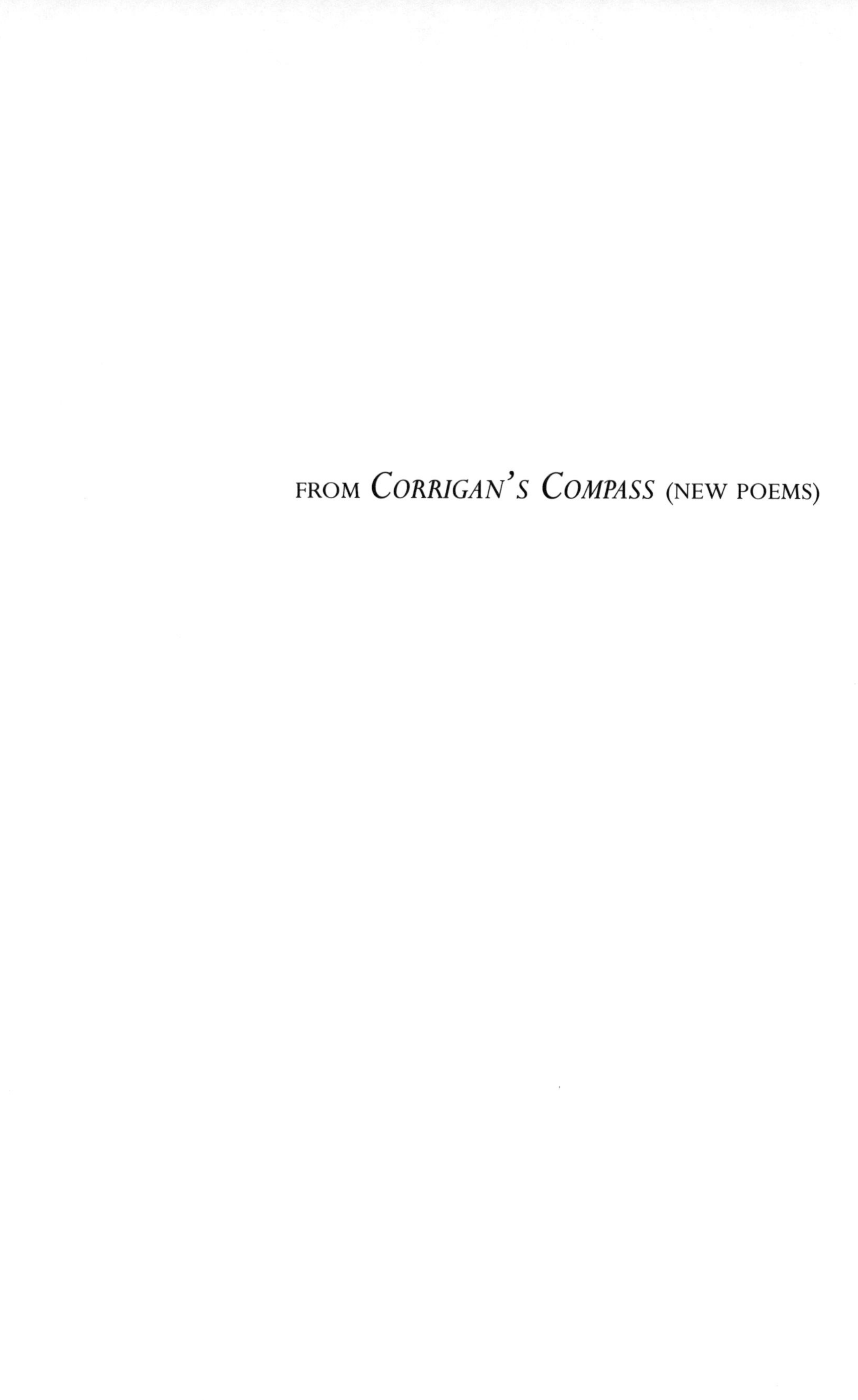

FROM *CORRIGAN'S COMPASS* (NEW POEMS)

SLEEP'S DARK AND SILENT GATE

I slept in the back of old television sets,
in cupboards, between the pages of dull books.
I slept for days, months. Every part of me
slept—limbs, feet, the tip of my tongue.
When I woke I could hardly speak,
my voice still asleep even as the muscles
inside my mouth shaped the air
and forced it out between my lips to make
the sounds others might hear.
When she was eight years old, my sister
slept in a hayloft and walked, at midnight,
out the loft door into nothing but moonlight,
trusting the radiant air to uphold her.
I heard rumors of those who could not sleep,
prisoners of night, pre-ghosts practicing
their age-old insomnia. But not me.
I slept at the bottom of cracked teacups.
I slept in unlabeled boxes in the basements
of abandoned houses. And once,
I slept in the hollow of my father's hand
waiting for the sun to touch his shoes,
the polished buckle of his belt,
the coins from his pocket tossed carelessly
onto the bureau near his wallet
and the picture of my mother,
slim as a schoolgirl, her eyes
dark with the heaviness of unknowing.
I slept waiting for some final illumination
and the day to begin.

ALL THAT WAS MEANT TO BRING US TOGETHER

This question comes up again and again
in our discussion group: am I the same person
I was when I was a child? And does
it matter if we catch ourselves making faces
at ourselves in the mirror when no one's watching?

In China, for $100, a "tomb sweeper" will clean
your parents' graves. He'll place fresh flowers there
and videotape the whole thing so you can see
what he's done and admire his work.

Grief by proxy is little more than a mannequin.

Even today I said "not now" to three Facebook
applicants; I'm such a vicious clicker.

It began innocently enough with the telephone
answering machine. Who now can imagine
a world without the net, the ubiquitous
cell phone sifting airwaves for the slightest hint
of interest from distant towers?

                  Yet that woman
I saw sleeping in a doorway is dead now
and the Press has forgotten the boy with no hands,
face peppered with shrapnel, as the sand
outside begins to shape itself into his future grave.

LONG BEACH AVENUE

We were only driving home, my mother at the wheel,
the three of us causing havoc in the back seat,
my mother's sharp exhortations to make us stop.
It was summer, hot tar sticky by the roadsides,
the trees along the avenue flush with leaves.

We were only driving home when we passed
the wreck, a car turned over on its side on someone's
lawn, its unseemly undercarriage exposed—
the policeman looking down at something covered
with a blanket, a small foot protruding, the people
huddled by the curb making an odd tableau.

We were only driving home when the boy's body
lay still under the blanket and his mother stood by,
her dress spotted with blood, my brother
and sister and I finally quiet at the strange sight
just around the corner from our house with the ancient elm
and the trellis with its bitter clusters of grapes.

We went inside and ate our dinner and went
to bed and the moon rose over the sleeping
avenues and the leaves rustled in a breeze
that came to us across the darkened ocean.

THE HIGH WIDE DOORS OF AMERICA

October arrived in a splash of rust.
Outside, certain growths on tree trunks
resembled women's breasts. A man told me
he hadn't been in the neighboring town,
only eleven miles away, for thirty years.
I was so lonely then, I believed him.
I'd drive from village to village
wondering what it would be like
to live in them, each with its bank
and grocery, its white steeple puncturing the sky.
The high, wide church doors
had pairs of doors above them that might
be opened "in case an Angel arrived."
I believed that too, imagining
its clumsy wings, the congregation aghast.
One night I stood in a potato field
somewhere in Rhode Island
as it began to rain. I had no idea
where I was going, and not much more about
how I'd gotten there. Is it possible
to lose years, the way we lose
an address or a watch, so we
can't be said to have lived in them at all?
I thought that rain might take
the shape of buildings centuries old
even if those buildings vanished.
Sometimes it snowed, and the world
grew smaller. I hoped that if that Angel arrived
I'd be there, my face tilted towards
the light, and if I could believe that,
I could believe anything.

ANOTHER MOONY LOVE POEM

The moon, we are told, inches closer each year,
but have you thought of those footprints
left there unmolested since the 1960s?
And that flag, stretched on wire filaments
to make it look as though it's flapping in the breeze?

The first thing we did there was a lie.

We don't even glance up now, any more
than I think about my friend
whom I betrayed, whose wife drifted into my arms
the way that capsule drifted across
empty space to land on an alien surface
of dust and cosmic debris waiting for a heartbeat.

I'm not proud of that, or the cheap
motels we hid in like make-believe houses,
convinced that love exonerated everything.

I've loved other women since then,
but from this distance it's impossible to see
what we left, falsely flying,
the imprint of every step etched into the surface,
perfect and imperishable.

MIXED IN A FUSION INDISTINGUISHABLE

It's when I realized that I didn't have to explain the world
that the world began to explain itself to me.

Those nights I stopped under a Douglas fir on Ute Avenue
and looked up into that starry black tower
until I could sense it was also looking down at me.

Mornings dark with snowfall, twilight
turned upside down so the day unwound backwards.

"Events," says Melville, "are mixed in a fusion indistinguishable."

Everything in the past exists at once:
the day I hit a home run, and the battle of Lepanto;
Prester John and the neighbor's dog, Queenie;
my report on the habits of honeybees, and the Edict of Worms.

Bees fly back to the hive and dance in a circle
to indicate where they've found nectar six miles away.

"I am stucco'd with quadrupeds and birds all over,"
roared Whitman in a rapture of evolutionary fervor.
I can almost hear his pen scratching out those words.

How far we come in a lifetime meant little to him.
He was gazing down the narrow end of time,
and he didn't travel far. Not by modern standards.

But there's a molecule of mine that's drifted here
from the 19th century, and a molecule of yours that Caesar
liked to scratch.

Inside that tree a hundred winters lay coiled,
a century's chronicle of cold.

And these are just the facts.

ROAD TRIP WITH STARS AROUND MY ANKLES

The new road runs along the old road. I can see it
still imprinted on the earth, not twenty feet away
as I drive west past silos and farmsteads, fruit stands and hogs.

Once in Kansas, I stood in a field so flat I watched
the stars on the horizon revolve around my ankles.

When will the cities meet? When will they spread until
there is a single city—avenue to avenue, coast to coast?

What we call "the country" is an undeveloped area
by the side of the road. There is no "country," there is no "road."
It's one big National Park, no longer the wilderness it was.

But the old world exists under the present world
the way an original painting exists under a newer one.

The animals know: their invisible trails cross
and re-cross our own like scars that have healed long ago.
Their country is not our country but a place of instinct and blood.

In Amarillo the wind tries to erase everything, even the future.
It swoops down to scrape the desert clean as a scapula.

Here among bones and bleached arroyos the sun leans
through my window at dawn to let me know
I'm not going anywhere. There's no more anywhere to go.

RETROSPECTIVE ON THE BODY

Once, when making love to a woman,
I felt myself convulse like a dog.
I drifted above her, while my body went to town.

In those days I gave my heart away
like it was a piece of bad meat.

The body inside the body, and the body
inside that, finds its way back
to a small cave under the hypothalamus

where paintings depict sex acts
on the walls of the Lupanar in Pompeii.

There are those who think love is a social concept
and the body a mere machine.

But in a tunnel halfway between
a monastery in France and a nearby nunnery:
the skeletons of dead babies.

Hundreds of them.

IS THERE ANYTHING ELSE I CAN HELP YOU WITH TODAY

Records topple,

       the Midwest melts, rippling through a scrim of heat

     as though it were an illusion

and not reality.

      Someone fries an egg on a shovel.

Someone else lights a cigarette on a brick.

       Each day, I commit an act

        of brutal indifference.

This morning, for instance, rebel forces reached the tree

        outside my window

and cried out at the expanding light.

        Next door, Mrs. Neiman

called softly to her cat, and the sprinklers at Mr. Cota's house

switched on according to schedule.

       The old emperor fled, and the city fell,

leaving behind an eight-year-old boy,

       scaffold of bones and protuberant eyes,

skin cracked as parchment from acute hunger.

        How easy it is

to write the words "fear" or "thirst"

      when they aren't written

in your own blood.

     And poetry only makes awareness more complete.

I worry about processed meat, and the fat content of butter.

I look inside the fridge to see if we are low on coffee,

        and whether

the lettuce I bought at the market last week has wilted.

     The secretary at the telephone company is pretty

and smiles at me as she accepts my check:

       Is there anything else I can help you with today?

I live as I have always lived,

 despite the pain of others, cowering in paradise,

     hoping the destruction doesn't notice I'm here.

GREAT HISTORICAL PERSPECTIVES

That was the year we lived in a dovecote
and I wore a sundial on my wrist. It was always 1342.
Soldiers drank blood out of their horse's necks
when they ran out of water, and wine was served
in a skull, because no one had invented the cup yet.

These were hardships. History is mostly that.
We live in the present which is another kind of history
without cobwebs, as the future is history without flesh.

Today several telephones rang at once,
in different parts of the city, and that was thrilling
because the city is usually quiet, not even a car horn
or a siren to break the long somnolence of history.

It's all around us and in us, even now when five gulls
flew by my window heading towards another part of history,
the part where they weren't a few minutes ago.

Bottles hadn't been invented yet, either.
It makes you wonder: what did they do before anything
was invented? They didn't have to invent caves,
they just found them, so even houses lay in the future
like an ambition for comfort they hadn't yet conceived.

But this isn't about history at all.
Have you guessed that by now? Or dovecotes.
It's about how heavy that sundial was on my wrist,
and how long a shadow it cast all the way into the future.

LORCA AND THE COPENHAGEN SCHOOL OF PHYSICS

No piece of paper can be folded in half
more than seven times. This may seem trivial
but isn't it as portentous and absolute as $E=MC^2$?

I think Lorca was wrong. Mystery inheres in this world
as much as any other, and the laws of Nature
are not as tidy as we once assumed.

Consider Heisenberg and his mind-numbing principle,
as old now as your grandmother's shoes,
or Schrödinger's cat, which is both alive and dead
at the same time, according to the Copenhagen school.

I don't pretend to understand any of this,
and there are newer theories that make these
look quaint as science proliferates its enigmas.

Imagination can invent remarkable things,
but it could never have imagined this world.

Look closely at anything, and the clouds
of impossibility gather, the world wriggles free
of our grasp, Nature coyly accommodates the observer.
If this is true, then what is true? Lorca
never had to contemplate how light is both particle
and wave.

What I know is as mysterious
and mundane as sitting across from you
here at a table under fruit trees on the first day
of fall. That such a thing is ordinary beggars
imagination; that we make light of it,
a mockery of the miraculous.
The commonest thing
coheres out of all time and space, which invests it
with a kind of grandeur we can't possibly comprehend.

Here. Take my hand. Tell me it isn't true.

THE GOLIATH BIRD-EATER VERSUS THE HUMAN HEART

The valves of the human heart
are as thick as a single piece of tissue paper.
Nothing but a cheap balloon.

Mild weather, then a plunge
in temperature. Sometimes, down
in the dark, I can't find my feelings
with a flashlight.

Rain tonight, so tentative it touches
the windows without leaving
any prints.
       No webs, no trap doors,
the bird-eating spider rushes straight
at anything that moves. I love
these metaphors that lie in wait,
hoping for a wayward mind to snatch them.

For example: elephants can remain
standing after they die. Who doesn't know
someone like that?
       Now the sky's divided, half
sunshine, half dark louring clouds.

It's the second largest spider in the world.
Of course, they eat their mates.
Who doesn't know someone like that?

It's like one of those horror story monsters,
the heart. You have to kill it, again
and again, before it will truly die.

Freud speaks of "the overestimation
of the erotic object." And there's the rub.

When threatened, it rubs its abdomen
with its hind legs to release poisonous hairs
that can cause severe irritation.

Then slowly, almost shyly, it begins to rain.

YOU HAVE BEEN FOUND WANTING

chalked on the sidewalk where I pass answers
the question I've been asking myself, as it would answer anyone's,
so open-ended is it—a rhetorical answer scuffed by the wind.

What a struggle I've had to resist knowing everything!
For example, Aeschylus died the most undignified of deaths
when an eagle dropped a turtle on his head in order to break it open.
                                        The turtle, that is.
        I tried knowing nothing for a while.
"I know nothing," I'd say, but it sounded hollow,
and I had to admit I knew something. I knew the universe doesn't supply
answers to our questions through cryptic signs or chalk
scrawled on pavement, cloud formations or the entrails of birds.

        O blessed rage for knowledge!
The world is a mirror in which we see ourselves projected
as we are mirrors in which we see the world.
I glance down at the sidewalk and wonder how I'm wanting, what defect
plagues me unawares.
                Poor Aeschylus, out for a stroll
when a dumb bird dropped a mindless amphibian
on one of the brainiest citizens of ancient Greece.

        How can we account for anything,
I want to scribble on the sidewalk next to that vague accusation.
But I keep walking, sure I'll get nowhere, and that it will have to be enough.

Other New Poems

TAKING A STEPDAUTHER TO COLLEGE

You have your own car, and I must follow you
over this long road to the coast. You're on your way

to college, an old one founded by the clergy
when this country was a parable of deserts,
a wilderness to cross on their thorny way to heaven.

Already you are leaving me behind,
swooping out past slow pokes and trucks,
as I take my place in a regular line.

Nearly twenty years ago, I came this way
not much older than you are now,
driven by a different need.

I remember almost nothing of these bare canyons
with their scorpions and crows,
these saintly Joshua trees living on ashes and fire.

I could tell you how this land was made—
each canyon falling grain by grain to the river—
how the universities of rock teach time
slowly turning their shadowy pages.

People tell me you're blooming,
and I think of that in this wasted place.
I think of your mother's hands, their tiny fissures
clogged with dirt from her garden,
her brilliant flowers nursed through winter.

Miles away a dust devil rises, spins madly on a single toe,
then lapses back into a dry pile.
Overhead a hawk scans cactus,
studying flaws in the infinite fractures of shale.

We pass a grand cathedral of stone,
its organpipes and pews,
broken tombs for the sleep of martyrs.

Now you almost disappear in the shimmer of distance,
that place where the present buckles
at its edges, then unravels to plunge abruptly into the future.

They're right, of course, the wise professors,
gardeners of the mind's beauty—
you're bright as a peony, flushed pink and dreaming.

Little blossom, never planted by me.

for Maelle

KARMA

In another life, she had been a high wire artist—
Belgrade, Prague, and once even in London—
poised above the anxious faces of Europe
in the nineteenth century. But now in her split-level
home outside Detroit, at the end of the twentieth:
the blisters and sore feet! The ruptured ankles
of a circus queen! And that day in Rome
her husband, a wheat merchant from Rhodes,
had beat her within an inch of her life
right there in the market before the grinning
hyenas of Empire. Now her thighbone
ground in the socket of her hip, like a mortar
and pestle, and she had to limp through
the grocery for her daily bread. She had caught
cold once, in England, in a furious wind off the sea,
a wind full of salt and ice, and now
her sinuses ran and her eyes puckered up
and turned red in the middle of July.
History diminished her, the eternal suffering
of the world. Each life she remembered
brought more misery—a legacy of ills
acquired through time—the Druid's concubine,
a serf's daughter in Wales. She had to practice
amnesia, walking through the bright boutiques
and malls of America, whispering
"This is who I am…This is who I am"
until her back straightened, her vision cleared,
her muscles grew long and relaxed
as she lifted one of her lovely arms
to finger another necklace bought on credit and time.

WHERE'S THE ZOO

"There" you said, pointing a finger beyond the *Centraal* train station in Antwerp, across a narrow square—"The zoo is *there,* and when I waited for the trains, I could hear the lions roar!" Now the city roars louder and it's not the same zoo you knew as a child: sleek cats in their blond fury, humped elephants trumpeting to the crowd, snakes entwined in their fluorescent houses. All of it gone, now, into your girlhood—water bison, shrieking parrots—the whole menagerie unstable as a dream.

But all the Flemings are out today, filling the streets and the wide plaza near the cathedral, under a beer-gold sun. The cafés are mobbed, the shops thronged, light under the trees leafy as lace. People sit footsore and dazed, watching the square. The great parade of passersby never stops: we love to watch each other going nowhere. Now the bells begin, claiming the air with their huge clappers, echoing back through centuries of old suffering and war. Why does everything vanish as though it *wanted* to be gone?

(Thinking of you, sweetheart, I hear the lions roar.)

PAN DEL MUERTO

In Mexico, they bake bread
for those who died—flat
little cakes they leave around the house
for a mother or father or a child
to find. The dead are living
like us, growing fat, paying their debts,
brushing their teeth on schedule.
Sometimes it's hard to make your way
across a room to shake someone's
hand or give them a drink. The dead
are always there, in their evening gowns
and tuxedos, expecting to be served—
asking for more crackers or champagne.
Just making love is a sacrilege!
The grandmother is there and the school
teacher and the delicate sister,
even those who are not yet born,
more innocent than babies. You get
up in the morning to comb your
hair and you are combing the brittle hair
of the dead, which goes on growing
like the eyelashes and the finger
nails, as if the body were the last
to know or simply stubborn.
And maybe that's what the cakes are for—
to nourish the vanity of the corpse,
who after all would like to look
as good as possible on such a great
occasion. Listen! You hear the leaves
cracking faintly at dusk, a tire humming
on dry pavement, the sound of water
rushing through a pipe? The dead
are hungry! You must take
your knives and bowls and go down
into the cellar; you must begin to chant

those old recipes you've been saving—
mixing your own blood with the dry
sand the dead grow fat on,
that the children of the dead roll
into loaves for you to eat—
for the dust that will eventually pass
entirely through you.

COLOPHON

I've Come This Far to Say Hello: Poems Selected and New, by Kurt Brown, was designed by Philip Memmer, using, for the cover, Bodoni and Perpetua fonts, and for the text, Perpetua. Manufacturing was by McNaughton & Gunn, Saline, Michigan.

This book was published with the generous support of the following individuals:

Ronald Abeles

Kathleen Aguero & Richard Hoffman

Tricia Asklar

Paul August

Jeanne M. Beaumont

Susan Berlin

Rosalind Brenner

Mary Brown

Nickole Brown

Barry Burchell

Christopher Bursk

Carol Owens Campbell

Regina Colonia Willner

Wyn Cooper

Charles Cote

Barbara Curtiss

Chris & Pamela Davis

Debra Kang Dean

Carol Decanio

Maelle De Schutter

Mathieu De Schutter & Sara Roahen

Linda Dessnet

Gregory Djanikian

George Drew

Stephen Dunn & Barbara Hurd

Elizabeth Edwards

Gloria (Bunny) Edwards

Richard Foerster

Joan Frank
Sarah Freligh
Dan Gerber
Nancy Gifford
Betsy Gilbert
Janlori Goldman
Judith Harris
Eileen Harrison
Nate & Steph Harrison
Thomas Patrick Healy
Catherine & Rob Hodges
Luci & Richard Janssen
David Jauss
Kate Johnson
Meg Kearney and Gabriel Parker
Richard & Christine Kravetz
Laurie Kutchins
Elizabeth Lara
Dallas Lee & Mary Lee
Eugenia Leigh
Anthony Leuzzi
Deena Linett
Margaret Lloyd
Perie Longo
Robert Lopez
Thomas Lux
Kathleen Lynch
Amy MacLennan
Grace Dane Mazur
Chloe Y. Miller
Wendy & Jimmy Mnookin
Peter Murphy
Anne-Marie Oomen
Dzvinia Orlowsky & Jay Hoffman
Enid Osborne & Green Poet Press
Marcia Pelletiere

Peg Quinn

Barbara Ras

Harry Reese

Martha Rhodes

John & Muriel Ridland

Katrina Roberts

Natasha Sajé

Sarabande Books

Harold Schechter & Kimiko Hahn

Myra Shapiro

Susan Shields

Seymour & Renee Sievert

Charles & Helen Simic

Faye Snider

Barry Spacks

Alison Stone

Holly Stone

Ellen Sullins

Lisa Taylor

Madeline Tiger

Arnold Tolentino & Michelle Chin

Robert Vaughan

Margo Viscusi

Jennifer Wallace

Thom Ward

Sterling Watson

Estha Weiner

Jonathan Wells

Jett Whitehead

Bruce and Jodie Willard

Marty L. Williams

Peter & Joan Wood

Baron & Janet Wormser

Wren Wynn

Lauren Yaffe

David Yoo

Shaun G. Young

ACKNOWLEDGMENTS AND DEDICATIONS

Return of the Prodigals (1999) and *More Things in Heaven and Earth* (2002) were published by Four Way Books, PO Box 535, Village Station, New York, NY 10014.

Fables from the Ark (2004) was published by CustomWords, P.O. Box 541106, Cincinnati, OH 45254-1106. It was named Winner of the CustomWords Poetry Prize.

Sincerest Flatteries (2007) was published by Tupulo Press, PO Box 1767, North Adams, MA 01247.

Future Ship (2007) and *No Other Paradise* (2010) were published by Red Hen Press, Pasadena CA.

The editors of this volume gratefully acknowledge their permission to republish.

"The Kiss," "How It Arrives," "Love Poem," and "Where's the Zoo," are for Laure-Anne Bosselaar.

"A Father's Joke" is for the author's sister, Gloria Edwards.

"White, Middle-Class, Male," "Melville at the Custom House," and "Stag Film," are for Stephen Dunn.

"A Moment" is for Marie Ouhrabka.

"Tomorrow and Tomorrow" is for Steve Huff.

"For Miklos Radnoti" is for Virginia Slachman.

ABOUT THE AUTHOR

Kurt Brown was founding director of the Aspen Writers' Conference and founding director of Writers' Conferences & Centers. He served on the board of Poets House in New York for six years.

He was the editor of *Drive, They Said: Poems about Americans and Their Cars* (1994), *Verse & Universe: Poems about Science and Mathematics* (1998), and co-editor with his wife, poet Laure-Anne Bosselaar, of *Night Out: Poems about Hotels, Motels, Restaurants & Bars* (1997). In addition, he was the editor of *The Measured Word: On Poetry & Science,* and a co-editor of the tribute anthology for the late William Matthews, *Blues for Bill.* He was also co-editor, with Harold Schechter of *Conversation Pieces: Poems that Talk to Other Poems* and *Killer Verse: Poems about Murder & Mayhem.*

He was the author of six chapbooks: *The Lance & Rita Poems,* which won the Sound Post Press competition; *Recension of the Biblical Watchdog,* which won the Anamnesis Poetry Chapbook Competition; *A Voice in the Garden: Poems of Sandor Tádjèck* published by Beyond Baroque; *Mammal News,* Pudding House Press; *Fables from the Ark,* which won the Woodland Press Poetry Chapbook Competition, and *Sincerest Flatteries: A Little Book of Imitations,* published by Tupelo Press in the Masters' Series.

His first full-length collection, *Return of the Prodigals,* and second collection, *More Things in Heaven and Earth,* were published by Four Way Books. A third collection, *Fables from the Ark,* which won the 2003 Custom Words Prize, was published by WordTech, and a fourth, *Future Ship,* was published by Red Hen Press, followed by a fifth volume, *No Other Paradise.* His newest collection, *Time~Bound,* was published by Tiger Bark Press.

His memoir, *Lost Sheep: A Portrait of Aspen in the '70s,* came out from Conundrum Press; and *Eating Our Words: Poets Share Their Favorite Recipes* is due out from Tupelo Press in 2014. With Laure-Anne Bosselaar he translated a book by Flemish poet Herman de Coninck, entitled *The Plural of Happiness.*

He taught poetry workshops and craft classes at Sarah Lawrence College, was a McEver Visiting Chair in Writing at Georgia Tech in Atlanta, Georgia and a visiting writer at Westminster College in Salt Lake City, Utah.

He passed away in Santa Barbara, California, in June, 2013.

MORE POETRY FROM TIGER BARK PRESS

After That, by Kathleen Aguero

Crossing the Yellow River, trans. Sam Hamill

Night Garden, by Judith Harris

Time~Bound, by Kurt Brown

Sweet Weight, by Kate Lynn Hibbard

The Gate at Visby, by Deena Linett

River of Glass, by Ann McGovern

Inside Such Darkness, by Virginia Slachman

Transfiguration Begins at Home, by Estha Weiner

The Solvay Process, by Martin Walls

A Pilgrim into Silence, by Karen Swenson